CONTENTS

Culinary Entrepreneurship	1
A Personal Note from the Author	3
Introduction	6
Chapter 1: The Culinary Entrepreneur's Mindset	12
Chapter 2: Trends and Opportunities in the Food Industry	19
Chapter 3: Exploring Business Models – From Restaurants to Food Trucks	27
Chapter 4: Conducting Market Research for Food Ventures	36
Chapter 5: Formulating a Winning Concept	45
Chapter 6: Business Plan Essentials for Food Entrepreneurs	55
Chapter 7: Funding Your Culinary Venture	65
Chapter 8: Financial Planning and Budgeting	74
Chapter 9: Navigating Legal and Regulatory Requirements	84
Chapter 10: Location Strategy for Food Businesses	94
Chapter 11: Kitchen and Equipment Essentials	104

Chapter 12: Sourcing Ingredients and Supplier Management	115
Chapter 13: Menu Development and Pricing Strategy	126
Chapter 14: Managing Inventory and Minimizing Waste	136
Chapter 15: Hiring and Training a Stellar Team	147
Chapter 16: Building a Brand in the Food Industry	158
Chapter 17: Digital Marketing for Culinary Ventures	168
Chapter 18: Customer Experience and Relationship Management	178
Chapter 19: Managing Reputation and Crisis Communications	188
Chapter 20: Developing a Loyalty Program and Retention Strategies	199
Chapter 21: Scaling Your Food Business	210
Chapter 22: Integrating Sustainable Practices	220
Chapter 23: Technology and Innovation in Food Entrepreneurship	230
Chapter 24: Preparing for the Future of Food Entrepreneurship	242
Conclusion	253
Epilogue	260
References	265
Glossary of Terms	268
Acknowledgments	274
Copyright Information	276

Disclaimer 277

CULINARY ENTREPRENEURSHIP

Starting And Managing Food Businesses

Author: Dr Bhaskar Bora

A PERSONAL NOTE FROM THE AUTHOR

Though laden with unexpected trials and hardships, my journey has blossomed into a story of profound transformation—a journey that has led me to discover purpose, not in the towering milestones of success, but in the quiet, tender moments of love, care, and presence. What you hold in your hands is not merely a collection of recipes, but a testament to resilience—a narrative stitched together with threads of struggle, acceptance, and, in time, renewal.

There was a time when the story of my life played out with certainty and clarity, like a symphony where each note was perfectly placed. As a Doctor, my days were woven with the pulse of life itself—healing, comforting, offering hope where none had been. I wore my white coat with pride, for it was not just a garment but a symbol of who I was. The work I did, and the lives I touched, gave meaning to my every breath. My identity was fused with my role as a healer as if I had been born to follow that path.

But life, with its intricate unpredictability, had other plans. In a single, unforeseen moment, the world I had so carefully built was undone—first with a spinal cord injury that took away the physical strength I had always known, and then with the looming shadow of cancer, a reminder of how fragile life truly is. The vibrant world of medicine, where I once found purpose and joy, suddenly slipped beyond my reach. What once was filled with meaning became a void, vast and silent, leaving me to ask the questions I never thought I would need to face.

The bustling hospital hallways were exchanged for the quiet solitude of my home, where I was no longer a "Doctor." My hands, once steady with the knowledge of healing, trembled in the face of an unknown future. Who was I without the title, the purpose, and the work that defined me? I stood at the edge of this new reality, uncertain and untethered, wondering what life could offer beyond what I had known.

In the silence of that transition, I discovered something

unexpected. What once seemed like an unfamiliar, distant role—being a disabled husband and a disabled father—became the essence of my existence. And within that shift, I found cooking. What began as an effort to nurture my family soon became a source of healing for me. In the rhythm of chopping, stirring, and tasting, I discovered a new purpose. Cooking became a language through which I reconnected with life, a practice that grounded me when everything else felt adrift and connected to the ones I love.

These past few years spent creating nourishing, simple meals, have been my lifeline—a daily practice of care for the people I love and for myself. Exploring different cuisines, experimenting with flavours, reading about ingredients and techniques—all of it became not just a pastime but a pathway to reclaiming my identity. Through cooking, I found a way forward, one meal at a time.

What I share with you now through this book, and those that will follow, are the lessons learned along the way. They are simple, practical, and grounded in love. These recipes and cooking tips are not adorned with glossy images or extravagant flourishes, but they carry with them the essence of resilience, creativity, and joy. I hope that they bring as much warmth and nourishment to your home as they have to mine, and that in their simplicity, you find a way to savour the moments spent with the ones you cherish.

We cannot control what the universe throws at us, but how we react to those curveballs defines who we are and what we make of our lives.

INTRODUCTION

Overview Of Culinary Entrepreneurship

Culinary entrepreneurship is more than simply starting a food business; it's a fusion of passion, creativity, resilience, and strategic thinking. In today's dynamic and competitive food industry, culinary entrepreneurs are those bold visionaries who see opportunity where others see a plate of food, who understand the profound cultural and economic impact of a single meal served to a customer, and who transform dining experiences into thriving businesses. Culinary entrepreneurship encompasses a diverse spectrum of ventures—from gourmet restaurants and bustling food trucks to pop-up stalls, catering companies, and innovative meal-kit services. This book is an in-depth exploration of this ever-evolving field, tailored for anyone who has dreamed of starting a food business and desires a practical, yet comprehensive guide to navigating the journey.

In every culture, food plays a fundamental role; it's a universal language that binds people together, transcends cultural boundaries, and fuels economic growth. Food businesses have always been foundational pillars of society, acting as cultural landmarks and essential sources of income. Whether a restaurant on a busy urban street corner, a humble food truck parked near a bustling event, or an artisanal bakery serving a local neighbourhood, each culinary venture contributes significantly to the vibrancy and identity of its locale. But beyond the ability to create an experience, food entrepreneurs serve as key economic players, supporting local farmers, suppliers, artisans, and the hospitality industry. This book provides not just the essential tools for launching and managing a food business but also insight into understanding and leveraging the social and economic importance of the culinary industry in a modern context.

Types of Food Businesses

In recent years, culinary entrepreneurship has diversified, offering a wide array of business models that cater to the varied tastes and lifestyles of today's consumers. Traditional restaurants—whether fine dining, casual, or fast-food—remain popular, yet many entrepreneurs are gravitating toward more flexible, cost-effective models that align with changing consumer demands. Food trucks, for example, have revolutionized the industry by providing chefs and owners a way to serve innovative cuisine without the high overhead of a physical location. Pop-up restaurants and seasonal food stalls add a sense of novelty and exclusivity, allowing entrepreneurs to test new concepts and gain customer feedback before committing to a permanent venture.

In addition to these physical spaces, food entrepreneurs are increasingly venturing into digital and hybrid models, such as meal delivery services and virtual restaurants, which operate exclusively through online orders. Other food ventures, like catering businesses, food halls, and shared kitchens, offer specialized services and are pivotal in helping communities thrive. Each model has unique requirements, challenges, and opportunities, which this book will dissect to offer a deep understanding of what it takes to succeed in each type of business.

Importance in the Modern Economy

The impact of food businesses extends beyond simply providing a service or a meal; they are vital contributors to both local and national economies. In many parts of the world, small and medium-sized food enterprises employ millions, from chefs and servers to delivery drivers and logistics coordinators. A successful restaurant or food truck doesn't only bring revenue to its owner; it creates jobs, stimulates local economies, and fosters other small businesses by sourcing locally-produced ingredients, collaborating with suppliers, and attracting visitors to the area. Food businesses often serve as incubators for creativity, encouraging culinary artists to experiment with flavours, techniques, and fusions that keep the industry fresh and relevant.

The economic landscape of food entrepreneurship is as rich as it is complex, influenced by trends like health consciousness, eco-friendly practices, and demand for culturally diverse cuisines. Each of these trends drives innovation, impacting everything from menu offerings to business operations. Consumers are increasingly seeking experiences that align with their values, such as sustainably sourced ingredients, plant-based options, and culturally authentic dining experiences. For entrepreneurs, this presents both a challenge and an opportunity to differentiate their businesses by aligning with these evolving consumer preferences. This book will guide readers in understanding how to capitalize on these trends, maintain relevance, and create unique value propositions that attract and retain loyal customers.

Structure of the Book

"Culinary Entrepreneurship: Starting and Managing Food Businesses" is organized into five comprehensive sections, each addressing a critical aspect of food entrepreneurship. The first section delves into the fundamentals, focusing on the entrepreneurial mindset essential for success in the culinary world, as well as emerging trends and diverse business models. Here, we'll explore the different paths available to food entrepreneurs and help you determine which aligns best with your vision, resources, and goals.

The second section tackles business planning and

financial management. Here, readers will learn to create a solid business plan that outlines their mission, identifies their target market, and presents a realistic financial forecast. We'll cover financing options, budgeting, and how to navigate the legal and regulatory landscape—everything an aspiring entrepreneur needs to establish a secure foundation for their venture.

In the third section, we'll focus on setting up and optimizing operations, covering key areas such as kitchen design, ingredient sourcing, menu development, and team management. Operational efficiency is crucial in the food industry, where margins are tight, and customer expectations are high. Practical strategies and case studies will be provided to offer insights on creating a seamless, cost-effective, and customer-focused operation.

Marketing and branding take centre stage in the fourth section, which will explore the strategies needed to build a loyal customer base, from social media engagement and digital marketing to cultivating a memorable in-store experience. This part will guide you in crafting a brand that resonates with your audience and stands out in a crowded marketplace, ultimately driving both customer loyalty and long-term success.

Finally, the fifth section addresses scaling, sustainability, and future trends. Growing a food business requires careful planning and adaptability, whether expanding to multiple locations, franchising, or launching new products. We'll also discuss the importance of sustainable practices, both environmentally and financially, as well as the technological innovations shaping the future of the food industry.

Each chapter is packed with detailed insights, real-world examples, and actionable advice designed to equip readers with the skills and knowledge to thrive in the world of culinary entrepreneurship. By the end of this book, you will not only have a thorough understanding of what it takes to launch and sustain a food business, but you'll also be ready to embrace the challenges and rewards that come with creating memorable, meaningful, and profitable food experiences.

CHAPTER 1: THE CULINARY ENTREPRENEUR'S MINDSET

The food industry is a complex and challenging arena that demands more than just culinary skill. Culinary entrepreneurship requires a unique blend of resilience, creativity, calculated risk-taking, and adaptability. Successful food entrepreneurs transform their passion into purpose, balancing artistry with business acumen while navigating a world where consumer tastes are ever-evolving, and market competition is fierce. This chapter explores the essential traits and skills that define successful culinary entrepreneurs, supported by real-life case studies from around the world. Each example demonstrates how emotional resilience, innovation, risk tolerance, and flexibility play critical roles in entrepreneurial success.

Essential Traits of a Culinary Entrepreneur

1. Emotional Resilience

The culinary industry is notorious for its high-stress environment. Entrepreneurs must learn to withstand intense pressure, manage setbacks, and persist through challenges. Emotional resilience—the ability to recover from difficulties and maintain motivation despite obstacles—is fundamental for long-term success. Studies highlight that resilient individuals are more likely to maintain a positive outlook and exhibit proactive coping strategies, crucial for managing the stresses of entrepreneurship (Hayward, Forster, Sarasvathy, & Fredrickson, 2010).

- Case Study: Pooja Rajan, Founder of Pooja's Plant-Based Kitchen

Pooja Rajan, a plant-based culinary entrepreneur in Mumbai, India, exemplifies resilience. She faced considerable challenges when launching her vegan catering business in a traditionally meat-heavy market. In the initial stages, Rajan encountered financial constraints, scepticism from consumers, and even supply chain issues as she sought sustainable, plant-based ingredients. Despite these setbacks, she persisted by focusing on community engagement, hosting free tasting events, and educating consumers on the health benefits of a plant-based diet. Today, Pooja's Plant-Based Kitchen has become a sought-after name in Mumbai's wellness community, known for its creative vegan dishes. Her story illustrates how resilience can help an entrepreneur overcome initial obstacles to build a successful venture.

2. Creativity and Innovation

Creativity in culinary entrepreneurship extends

beyond inventing dishes; it involves problem-solving, strategic branding, and envisioning a concept that appeals to target customers. Innovation, which includes introducing new flavours, techniques, and dining experiences, is essential to creating a brand that stands out in a crowded market. Research has shown that creativity is especially critical in industries where differentiation is key, such as food service, where new trends emerge frequently (Amabile, 1996).

- Case Study: Ahmed Mansoor, Owner of Spice Caravan

Ahmed Mansoor, a culinary entrepreneur based in London, founded Spice Caravan, a fusion food truck that blends North African and Middle Eastern flavours. Recognizing the growing interest in street food and the public's enthusiasm for unique, authentic flavours, Mansoor saw an opportunity to combine elements of his heritage with modern British street food culture. His signature dish—a couscous wrap with lamb kofta, caramelized onions, and pomegranate sauce—quickly gained popularity. Mansoor's creative approach to blending flavours and presenting traditional ingredients in a contemporary format set his business apart, illustrating the role of creativity and innovation in attracting a loyal customer base.

3. Risk Tolerance

Culinary entrepreneurship is inherently risky, from financial investment to market reception. Entrepreneurs must be comfortable with uncertainty and ready to take calculated risks. Successful food entrepreneurs understand that bold actions—launching a new concept, investing in high-quality ingredients, or opening a location in an untapped area—are often necessary for growth. Research highlights that individuals with high risk tolerance tend to approach challenges proactively, which is crucial in the dynamic food industry (Cantillon, 1755; Baron, 2007).

- Case Study: Luisa Romero, Co-Founder of La Casa de Arepas

Originally from Caracas, Venezuela, Luisa Romero brought her love for Venezuelan cuisine to Miami, Florida. Together with her business partner, she co-founded La Casa de Arepas, a restaurant specializing in arepas, a traditional Venezuelan cornmeal dish. Romero faced the challenge of entering a highly competitive market filled with diverse food options. She took a calculated risk by investing in a high-traffic location and focusing on authenticity, importing specific ingredients to maintain the flavour profile of traditional arepas. Her gamble paid off, as La Casa de Arepas became popular not only among Venezuelan expatriates but also with locals and tourists eager for an authentic Latin American dining experience. Romero's journey underscores how calculated risks, rooted in a strong vision, can lead to entrepreneurial success.

4. Adaptability and Flexibility

In an industry where consumer preferences, regulations, and competition are constantly evolving, adaptability is an essential trait for culinary entrepreneurs. Those who can adjust their menus, marketing strategies, or operational processes in response to new demands often maintain a competitive edge. Studies emphasize that adaptability is a strong predictor of success in industries like food service, where rapid responses to market changes are crucial (Pulakos et al., 2000).

  - Case Study: Ji-Ho Park, Owner of Seoul Street Bites

Ji-Ho Park's adaptability has been key to his success as the owner of Seoul Street Bites, a Korean street food restaurant in Sydney, Australia. Initially focused on a dine-in experience, Park quickly pivoted to a delivery-first model when the COVID-19 pandemic forced restaurants to close their doors. He adapted his menu to include dishes that travelled well, such as Korean fried chicken and bibimbap bowls. This flexibility allowed Seoul Street Bites to continue operating during challenging times and even grow its customer base as delivery orders increased. Park's story exemplifies how adaptability can turn a potential crisis into an opportunity for growth and innovation.

Developing the Mindset for Success

Building these traits requires a commitment to continuous learning and self-improvement. While some may possess these qualities naturally, many successful culinary entrepreneurs have developed resilience, creativity, risk tolerance, and adaptability through experience, mentorship, and self-reflection.

- Resilience can be cultivated through practices such as mindfulness and stress management, which help entrepreneurs remain focused during challenging periods. Research indicates that emotionally resilient individuals are more likely to cope effectively with stress, allowing them to make sound decisions under pressure (Kabat-Zinn, 2003).

- Creativity can be nurtured by embracing diverse culinary traditions, exploring various culinary techniques, and engaging in brainstorming sessions with other industry professionals. According to Amabile (1996), creativity is often a product of exposure to new ideas and diverse perspectives.

- Risk Tolerance grows with a deeper understanding of the culinary landscape and the development of a strong support network. Conducting thorough market research and establishing contingency plans can help entrepreneurs make bold moves while minimizing potential setbacks.

- Adaptability requires maintaining a growth mindset, viewing change as an opportunity rather than a threat. Studies suggest that individuals with high psychological flexibility are better equipped to adjust to shifting demands, leading to improved stress management and decision-making abilities (Roberts, Dutton, Spreitzer, Heaphy, & Quinn, 2005).

The Mindset for Culinary Success

The stories of Pooja Rajan, Ahmed Mansoor, Luisa Romero, and Ji-Ho Park illustrate the mindset of successful culinary entrepreneurs. Each of them faced unique challenges and uncertainties, yet they persevered by developing resilience, leveraging creativity, taking calculated risks, and adapting to change. These real-life examples underscore the importance of a strong, dynamic mindset for anyone entering the food industry.

As the journey of these entrepreneurs shows, success

in culinary entrepreneurship requires more than just culinary skill or financial resources. It calls for a mindset rooted in resilience, innovation, courage, and flexibility. This chapter lays the foundation for understanding the psychological framework of successful culinary entrepreneurs. The following chapters will delve into the practical steps of launching and managing a food business, but it is this mindset that underpins every successful venture.

As readers move forward in their culinary journeys, they should embrace the lessons from these entrepreneurs—recognizing that, while the path may be challenging, the rewards of building a thriving food business that reflects their passion and values are unparalleled.

CHAPTER 2: TRENDS AND OPPORTUNITIES IN THE FOOD INDUSTRY

In recent years, the food industry has undergone rapid transformation, fuelled by changing consumer preferences, technological advancements, and a growing awareness of environmental and health concerns. Culinary entrepreneurs must navigate an industry in which trends evolve constantly, yet each new development brings with it a wealth of opportunities. This chapter explores three significant trends—sustainability, plant-based diets, and fusion cuisine—and examines how these trends provide unique avenues for new food ventures. By understanding the demographic and economic factors driving these shifts, culinary entrepreneurs can position their businesses to thrive in a competitive, dynamic market.

Understanding Key Trends in the Food Industry

1. Sustainability: Building a Greener Future for Food

The concept of sustainability has become central to the modern food industry, driven by concerns about climate change, environmental degradation, and resource scarcity. Consumers are increasingly aware of the ecological footprint of their food choices, and they expect businesses to adopt sustainable practices. According to the Food and Agriculture Organization (FAO), the global food system is responsible for approximately one-third of greenhouse gas emissions, primarily from meat and dairy production, deforestation, and food waste (FAO, 2020). As a result, sustainability in food businesses is no longer optional—it has become a fundamental expectation.

Sustainability in the food industry encompasses various practices, including sourcing locally, reducing waste, minimizing energy usage, and choosing sustainable packaging. For example, many restaurants now source their ingredients from local farmers to reduce transportation emissions and support regional agriculture. Others have adopted zero-waste practices, where food scraps are repurposed, and kitchen operations are optimized to reduce waste.

- Opportunities in Sustainable Practices

Culinary entrepreneurs can capitalize on the sustainability trend by incorporating eco-friendly practices into their business models. For instance, starting a zero-waste café or a farm-to-table restaurant can attract environmentally conscious consumers willing to support businesses that align with their values. Additionally, sustainable packaging options, such as biodegradable containers or reusable containers for takeout, offer a way to differentiate a food business. According to a survey by Nielsen (2018), 73% of consumers said they would change their consumption habits to reduce environmental impact, and this statistic underscores the demand for sustainable dining options.

- Case Study: Alice Waters and Chez Panisse

Chef Alice Waters is often credited with pioneering the farm-to-table movement through her renowned restaurant Chez Panisse in Berkeley, California. Since its inception in the 1970s, Chez Panisse has emphasized using locally sourced, organic ingredients and has inspired countless restaurants worldwide to adopt similar practices. Waters' commitment to sustainable, seasonal cooking not only made Chez Panisse an iconic establishment but also highlighted the economic and environmental benefits of local sourcing. Her example demonstrates how a focus on sustainability can establish a unique brand identity and attract a dedicated customer base.

2. The Rise of Plant-Based Diets

The shift towards plant-based diets is one of the most profound transformations in consumer eating habits. Driven by health consciousness, environmental concerns, and animal welfare issues, plant-based foods have moved from niche markets to mainstream menus. A 2021 report by The Good Food Institute revealed that plant-based food sales in the United States reached $7 billion, growing nearly twice as fast as total food sales

(GFI, 2021). This trend is fuelled by consumers seeking healthier, more sustainable alternatives to animal-based products, and it has created substantial opportunities for food entrepreneurs.

Plant-based diets are no longer limited to vegans and vegetarians; many consumers identify as "flexitarians," meaning they primarily eat plant-based foods but still consume animal products occasionally. This flexibility has led to the proliferation of innovative plant-based products, such as meat substitutes, dairy-free alternatives, and protein-rich grains, making it easier for restaurants and food businesses to integrate plant-based options into their offerings.

- Opportunities in the Plant-Based Market

For culinary entrepreneurs, the rise of plant-based diets offers a chance to capture a broad customer base by offering plant-centric menus or dedicated plant-based establishments. Restaurants can experiment with unique vegetable-forward dishes, or develop fusion cuisine that caters to the plant-based trend while providing familiar flavours. Entrepreneurs who focus on health benefits, flavour innovation, and sustainability can appeal to health-conscious and environmentally aware consumers. Additionally, pop-up plant-based kitchens or food trucks provide low-risk ways to test plant-based concepts before committing to a full-scale operation.

- Case Study: Pinky Cole and Slutty Vegan

Pinky Cole, the founder of Slutty Vegan, exemplifies how a plant-based business can achieve mainstream success. Based in Atlanta, Slutty Vegan serves indulgent, plant-based fast food with a fun, provocative branding approach. Cole's business model broke the mould by positioning plant-based food as fun and accessible rather than restrictive. Slutty Vegan's popularity has skyrocketed, attracting celebrities and a diverse clientele eager to try vegan burgers with a twist. Cole's success demonstrates the potential of plant-based entrepreneurship to tap into new customer demographics and create a strong brand identity.

3. Fusion Cuisine: Blending Flavours and Cultures

Fusion cuisine, which combines elements from diverse culinary traditions, has been a popular trend for decades but continues to evolve as globalization increases and cross-cultural culinary exchanges flourish. Fusion cuisine allows chefs to experiment with unique combinations of flavours, techniques, and ingredients, often resulting in dishes that resonate with a broad audience. This trend is particularly popular among younger consumers who are open to trying new foods and appreciate innovative dining experiences.

The success of fusion cuisine can be attributed to its adaptability and potential for creativity. With the rise of global tourism, migration, and media exposure to international food, consumers are increasingly familiar with and open to different culinary traditions. As a result, fusion cuisine presents an opportunity for culinary entrepreneurs to cater to adventurous palates by merging familiar flavours with exotic elements.

- Opportunities in Fusion Cuisine

Culinary entrepreneurs can leverage fusion cuisine to create unique, signature dishes that set their business apart from the competition. Food trucks, pop-up events, and fusion-inspired menus are popular avenues for testing new flavour combinations. Fusion cuisine also appeals to multicultural communities and travellers looking for novel dining experiences that reflect the diversity of global food culture.

- Case Study: Roy Choi and Kogi BBQ

Roy Choi, a Korean-American chef, revolutionized the food truck industry with his creation of Kogi BBQ, a fusion of Korean and Mexican flavours. Choi's signature dish, the Korean BBQ taco, became an instant hit in Los Angeles and quickly garnered a cult following. By combining the flavours of his heritage with the street food culture of LA, Choi introduced fusion cuisine to a new generation of consumers. His success highlights how fusion cuisine can captivate audiences by blending authenticity with innovation, offering a model for entrepreneurs seeking to create unique, culturally rich food experiences.

Demographic and Economic Influences on Consumer Choices

Understanding the demographic and economic factors that influence consumer food choices is essential for culinary entrepreneurs aiming to capitalize on current trends. These factors shape preferences and spending habits, making it crucial for entrepreneurs to adapt their offerings to meet the needs of their target audience.

1. Generational Preferences

Millennials and Gen Z are the driving forces behind many food industry trends, particularly those centred on health, sustainability, and innovation. According to Forbes, 87% of millennials are willing to spend more on sustainable products, and they often prioritize experiences over material goods, making them a prime market for unique and eco-conscious food ventures (Forbes, 2019). Gen Z, meanwhile, values diversity and inclusivity, often seeking brands that align with their social values.

2. Health Consciousness

Increasing awareness of health and wellness is another major driver of consumer behaviour. The rise of chronic health issues, such as obesity and diabetes, has led consumers to seek healthier food options. Demand for organic, minimally processed, and nutrient-dense foods has grown significantly, creating a space for entrepreneurs to introduce healthier alternatives to traditional fast food.

3. Economic Factors

Economic conditions also influence consumer food choices, particularly when it comes to discretionary spending. In times of economic downturn, consumers may seek budget-friendly dining options, and businesses that can offer high-quality meals at affordable prices are likely to thrive. During periods of economic growth, consumers may be more willing to splurge on premium or gourmet dining experiences. Entrepreneurs must be able to adjust pricing strategies and menu offerings based on economic conditions, ensuring that their business remains viable.

Navigating Trends for Entrepreneurial Success

The food industry is a landscape of continuous innovation and reinvention, shaped by trends that reflect the evolving values and desires of society. Sustainability, plant-based diets, and fusion cuisine are three powerful trends that offer extensive opportunities for culinary entrepreneurs to establish unique brands, connect with consumers, and make a meaningful impact. By embracing sustainable practices, offering plant-based options, or creating fusion-inspired menus, food businesses can cater to a wide array of customers who prioritize health, environmental responsibility, and culinary adventure.

As we have seen in the stories of Alice Waters, Pinky Cole, and Roy Choi, successful culinary entrepreneurs are those who understand these trends and adapt their businesses to align with the values of their target audience. Waters' commitment to sustainability, Cole's bold approach to plant-based comfort food, and Choi's innovative fusion of Korean and Mexican flavours all illustrate how understanding and capitalizing on trends can lead to a thriving food business. Each of these entrepreneurs has not only achieved commercial success but has also contributed to a broader movement within the food industry.

The trends and opportunities explored in this chapter represent more than fleeting consumer preferences; they reflect deep societal shifts that will continue to shape the future of the food industry. As culinary entrepreneurs consider their path forward, they must remain attuned to these shifts, continuously innovating and adapting to meet the demands of a new generation of consumers.

CHAPTER 3: EXPLORING BUSINESS MODELS – FROM RESTAURANTS TO FOOD TRUCKS

Choosing the right business model is one of the most crucial decisions a culinary entrepreneur will make. Each model, whether it's a traditional restaurant, a food truck, a catering service, or a pop-up, comes with its own unique set of advantages, challenges, and operational requirements. For aspiring food entrepreneurs, understanding these distinctions is essential to making an informed decision that aligns with their vision, financial capabilities, and target market.

In this chapter, we will explore various food business models, examining their differences, unique factors, and the risks and rewards associated with each. By the end of this discussion, aspiring culinary entrepreneurs will have a clearer understanding of which model best suits their goals and circumstances.

Types of Food Business Models

1. Traditional Restaurants

Traditional restaurants, whether fine dining, casual dining, or quick-service, have long been a cornerstone of the food industry. They offer a controlled environment, allowing entrepreneurs to curate the entire customer experience, from ambiance to service. Restaurants typically require a significant investment in location, interior design, and kitchen equipment. Moreover, they rely on a steady flow of customers and need strong branding and marketing to attract and retain patrons.

- Fine Dining: Fine dining establishments focus on delivering a high-end experience with premium ingredients, sophisticated service, and luxurious ambiance. Chefs in fine dining often have specialized training, and the dishes tend to reflect high levels of culinary creativity and artistry. This model, while prestigious, is also one of the most expensive to launch and operate, with high costs for location, staffing, and ingredients.

- Casual Dining: Casual dining provides a more relaxed atmosphere with moderately priced meals. This model appeals to a wider demographic, balancing quality food with affordability. Casual dining restaurants often rely on loyal repeat customers and can thrive in both urban and suburban locations.

- Quick-Service and Fast Food: Quick-service

restaurants (QSR) are designed for efficiency, offering simple menus, quick turnaround times, and low prices. This model is highly scalable and can be incredibly profitable if a strong brand is established. However, competition is fierce, and success often depends on location and brand recognition.

  - Case Study: Danny Meyer and Shake Shack

Restaurateur Danny Meyer launched Shake Shack as a hot dog cart in New York City's Madison Square Park, intending it as a casual and accessible extension of his fine dining background. The concept evolved into a chain of modern "fast-casual" burger restaurants, renowned for quality ingredients and an upscale take on classic American fast food. Shake Shack's expansion highlights the potential for scaling a restaurant when the model balances quality, branding, and efficiency. Meyer's success also underscores the importance of choosing a business model that aligns with both the entrepreneur's brand and market demand.

2. Food Trucks

Food trucks have gained immense popularity in recent years as a lower-cost, mobile alternative to traditional restaurants. With the ability to reach customers at different locations, food trucks offer unparalleled flexibility. For chefs and culinary entrepreneurs with limited startup capital, a food truck can be an ideal entry point, allowing them to build a following without the financial burden of a fixed location. Moreover, food trucks appeal to consumers looking for unique, on-the-go dining experiences.

  - Advantages: Lower startup costs, flexibility in

location, ability to test and refine the menu, and a strong appeal to urban, trend-focused consumers.

- Challenges: Permitting and licensing can be complex, weather affects sales, and storage space is limited.

- Target Market: Often appeals to younger consumers who are open to trying new, trendy foods and enjoy the convenience of mobile dining.

- Case Study: Veronica Garcia and Tacos Don Chente

Veronica Garcia launched Tacos Don Chente in Los Angeles as a family-owned food truck specializing in authentic Mexican street food. Operating in an area saturated with restaurants, Garcia chose the food truck model to reduce overhead costs and target customers in high-traffic locations like festivals, university campuses, and business districts. Tacos Don Chente's popularity grew rapidly due to its focus on traditional flavours and convenient locations, eventually leading to enough revenue to open a brick-and-mortar restaurant. Garcia's journey illustrates how a food truck can serve as a launchpad for growth and a testing ground for a culinary concept.

3. Catering Services

Catering businesses provide food for events, such as weddings, corporate gatherings, and private parties, rather than operating out of a fixed location. This model appeals to chefs who enjoy working with varied menus and customer requirements. Catering can be highly lucrative, with fewer overhead costs than a traditional restaurant and the flexibility to scale up or down based on the number of events booked. However, success in catering requires excellent organizational skills, as the logistics of preparing, transporting, and serving food at different venues can be complex.

- Advantages: Lower overhead, flexible schedule, ability to customize menus, and high-profit potential per event.

- Challenges: Inconsistent income, high competition, and the need for strong logistical and planning skills.

- Target Market: Events, corporate clients, and individuals seeking customized menus and professional food service.

- Case Study: Priya Singh and Flavours of India Catering

Priya Singh, an Indian chef based in Toronto, started Flavours of India Catering to bring authentic Indian cuisine to events in the city. Catering allowed Singh to showcase her culinary expertise without the need for a fixed restaurant space. She customized her services to meet the needs of diverse clients, from intimate family gatherings to large corporate events. By delivering consistently high-quality food and tailoring menus to client preferences, Flavours of India quickly gained a reputation for excellence. Singh's story demonstrates how catering offers a flexible business model that allows culinary entrepreneurs to earn substantial revenue while building a unique brand.

4. Pop-Up Restaurants

Pop-up restaurants are temporary dining experiences that often operate in unconventional locations, such as art galleries, rooftops, or even private homes. This model allows chefs to experiment with new concepts, showcase seasonal menus, and create a sense of exclusivity. Pop-ups are popular among culinary entrepreneurs who want to test a concept before committing to a permanent location or who seek to create buzz around a particular culinary event. This model typically involves short-term leases or collaboration with existing venues, making it a low-risk way to generate interest and gauge customer response.

- Advantages: Low startup costs, flexibility, ability to test concepts, and a sense of novelty that attracts curious customers.

- Challenges: Temporary nature, limited seating, dependency on effective marketing, and sometimes high setup costs for specific locations.

- Target Market: Food enthusiasts seeking unique experiences, often from younger demographics willing to pay a premium for novelty.

- Case Study: Ayesha Javed and "Spice Route" Pop-Up Series

Chef Ayesha Javed launched the "Spice Route" pop-up series to showcase the flavours of the Middle East and North Africa in New York City. Hosting pop-up dinners in various venues, Javed created an immersive experience by pairing her dishes with live music, storytelling, and culturally inspired decor. The temporary nature of Spice Route made it exclusive, generating word-of-mouth buzz and attracting a loyal following. Javed's approach to pop-ups highlights the potential of this model to build brand recognition and create memorable experiences without the long-term commitment of a permanent restaurant.

Factors to Consider When Choosing a Food Business Model

Each business model presents unique opportunities and challenges. Entrepreneurs should consider several factors when deciding which model best suits their goals and resources.

1. Initial Investment and Overhead Costs

The startup costs vary widely between models. Traditional restaurants, especially fine dining, require significant capital for location, renovations, and equipment, whereas food trucks and pop-ups offer lower-cost entry points. Catering businesses also have lower overheads but may require investment in transportable equipment and high-quality ingredients to meet client expectations.

2. Location Flexibility

Location flexibility is a defining factor for mobile models like food trucks and pop-ups. Traditional restaurants depend on a fixed location, making it critical to choose areas with high foot traffic or a target demographic. Food trucks, on the other hand, can capitalize on different locations to capture diverse customer bases, from urban lunch crowds to festival-goers.

3. Target Market and Demographic

Identifying the target market is essential when selecting a business model. A quick-service restaurant or food truck may appeal to younger, urban consumers, while fine dining is likely to attract an older, affluent demographic. Catering businesses often cater to corporate clients or high-income individuals, while pop-ups appeal to adventurous food enthusiasts.

4. Scalability

Some models, like food trucks and pop-ups, are highly scalable and can expand quickly with low capital. Traditional restaurants are often harder to scale due to high fixed costs, but if successful, they may open additional locations or franchise.

5. Operational Complexity

Each model varies in operational complexity. Catering requires meticulous planning and adaptability for different events, while pop-ups need creative setups in temporary locations. Food trucks, although mobile, come with logistical challenges like limited kitchen space and dependency on weather.

Comparative Analysis of Risks and Rewards in Food Business Formats

Each business model has distinct risks and rewards, and entrepreneurs must weigh these factors carefully:

- Traditional Restaurants: High financial risk due to substantial upfront investment and operating costs. However, if successful, restaurants can offer high profit margins and a loyal customer base.

- Food Trucks: Lower financial risk with flexibility, but vulnerable to external factors like weather and seasonal fluctuations. Can generate high rewards if strategically located and branded effectively.

- Catering Services: Low financial risk with flexible scheduling, but requires strong organizational skills. Offers high profit per event but depends on a consistent client base.

-

Pop-Up Restaurants: Low financial risk and flexible, with potential to generate buzz. However, temporary nature limits revenue potential and requires ongoing marketing efforts to maintain visibility.

Choosing the Right Model for Success

The choice of business model will significantly influence the direction of a food entrepreneur's journey. By assessing each model's unique characteristics, understanding the target market, and weighing the risks and rewards, aspiring culinary entrepreneurs can make informed decisions that align with their goals and resources. As seen in the stories of Danny Meyer, Veronica Garcia, Priya Singh, and Ayesha Javed, each model has the potential for success when matched with the right vision, market, and strategy.

Moving forward, aspiring culinary entrepreneurs can apply these insights to select the model that best complements their personal strengths, financial resources, and the experience they wish to create for their customers. Whether they choose the stable structure of a restaurant, the flexibility of a food truck, the event-focused nature of catering, or the creative allure of a pop-up, each path offers a unique opportunity to succeed in the dynamic world of food entrepreneurship.

CHAPTER 4: CONDUCTING MARKET RESEARCH FOR FOOD VENTURES

Understanding the market is foundational to the success of any food venture. In the crowded and highly competitive food industry, it's not enough to simply offer good food; entrepreneurs need to cater specifically to the tastes, preferences, and expectations of their target audience. Market research is the key to this understanding. It provides insights into consumer preferences, reveals opportunities in the market, and helps entrepreneurs define a unique value proposition (UVP) that differentiates their business from the competition. This chapter explores the importance of market research in food ventures, introduces effective tools and strategies for gathering data, and demonstrates how to use these insights to craft a compelling UVP.

The Importance of Understanding the Target Market

Market research enables entrepreneurs to tailor their offerings to meet the needs and desires of their target audience, making their businesses more likely to succeed. For example, a restaurant aiming to attract health-conscious millennials will require a different approach from one targeting families looking for affordable dining options. Understanding these distinct customer segments helps in creating a brand that resonates and meets specific expectations.

According to Harvard Business Review, businesses that conduct thorough market research are significantly more likely to achieve higher customer satisfaction and retention rates (Kotler, 2017). In the food industry, where consumer preferences can change rapidly, staying attuned to these shifts can make the difference between success and failure. Additionally, a well-defined target market allows businesses to allocate resources more efficiently, focusing their marketing, menu design, and service style on the specific needs of their audience.

Tools and Strategies for Gathering Market Data

There are several reliable methods for gathering market data, each offering unique insights into consumer behaviour and preferences. While each method has its strengths and limitations, using a combination of these tools can provide a comprehensive understanding of the market.

1. Surveys

Surveys are one of the most commonly used methods for gathering quantitative data about consumer preferences. They can be distributed online, through social media, in-store, or via email, making them accessible and cost-effective. Surveys allow businesses to ask specific questions about demographics, dining habits, and customer expectations. For example, a survey might ask customers how frequently they dine out, their preferred cuisines, or their opinion on sustainable packaging. The structured format of surveys makes it easy to analyse responses and identify trends within the target market.

- Example: Shake Shack's Customer Feedback Surveys

Shake Shack regularly conducts customer feedback surveys to better understand their patrons' needs and improve their dining experience. By asking questions related to menu preferences, service quality, and location convenience, Shake Shack gathers valuable data to guide operational improvements. For instance, if surveys indicate that customers desire healthier options, the restaurant can consider adding more nutritious choices to the menu. This responsiveness to customer feedback has helped Shake Shack grow and adapt to changing consumer preferences.

2. Focus Groups

Focus groups involve gathering a small group of potential customers to discuss their perceptions, preferences, and attitudes toward a product or concept. This method allows for in-depth exploration of consumer behaviour, as participants can elaborate on their opinions, preferences, and expectations in an open discussion. Focus groups are particularly useful for testing new menu items, branding concepts, or service ideas before they are launched on a larger scale.

- Example: McDonald's New Product Testing

McDonald's uses focus groups extensively to test new products and menu items before introducing them to the public. For instance, when developing their McPlant line of plant-based burgers, McDonald's gathered small groups of target consumers to provide feedback on taste, texture, and overall appeal. The insights from these discussions helped McDonald's refine the product and messaging to ensure it met the expectations of both meat-eaters and vegetarians. Focus groups offer valuable qualitative insights, allowing food ventures to adjust based on real consumer reactions.

3. Competitor Analysis

Competitor analysis involves studying the market offerings, strengths, and weaknesses of other businesses within the same segment. This method helps food entrepreneurs identify gaps in the market and understand how to differentiate their offerings. By examining competitors' menus, pricing, location, marketing tactics, and customer reviews, entrepreneurs can gain insights into what appeals to customers and where they can improve.

- Example: Comparing Local Food Trucks

A new food truck entrepreneur looking to serve fusion cuisine in a competitive urban area might analyse nearby food trucks offering similar options. By observing which trucks attract the most customers, what dishes are popular, and how these competitors engage with customers, the entrepreneur can refine their own concept to stand out. Perhaps they identify a gap in the market for fusion tacos with unique international flavours or see an opportunity to improve on competitors' customer service. Competitor analysis allows new businesses to capitalize on competitors' weaknesses and build a distinct brand.

4. Social Media Analytics

Social media platforms provide a wealth of data on consumer behaviour, preferences, and trends. By analysing metrics like engagement rates, comments, and shares, food ventures can gauge customer interest in various topics and gain insights into emerging trends. Platforms like Instagram and Facebook offer analytics tools that allow businesses to track which types of posts resonate most with their audience, helping to inform content and marketing strategies.

- Example: Café Gratitude's Social Media Insights

Café Gratitude, a plant-based restaurant chain in California, leverages social media analytics to understand what resonates with its health-conscious customer base. By monitoring the engagement on posts about new vegan dishes, sustainable practices, or community events, the café can determine which aspects of its brand appeal most to its audience. For example, if posts about seasonal produce receive high engagement, the restaurant might prioritize seasonal ingredients in its menu. Social media analytics thus provide real-time feedback on customer preferences and help refine marketing strategies.

Applying Market Research to Define a Unique Value Proposition (UVP)

A unique value proposition (UVP) is the statement that

defines what sets a business apart from competitors and why customers should choose it. In the food industry, where many businesses offer similar dishes or services, a strong UVP can be the key to attracting and retaining customers. Insights gathered from market research allow food ventures to develop a UVP that speaks directly to the needs and desires of their target market, making their brand memorable and compelling.

1. Identifying Customer Needs

By understanding the specific needs of their target market, entrepreneurs can create a UVP that directly addresses those needs. For example, if research reveals that customers in a given area are highly health-conscious, a café might position itself as the go-to spot for organic, locally sourced meals. By aligning the UVP with customer values, the business becomes more relevant and appealing.

- Example: Sweetgreen's UVP in the Healthy Eating Space

Sweetgreen, a fast-casual salad chain, has built a UVP around providing fresh, locally sourced, and customizable salads for health-conscious consumers. Through market research, Sweetgreen recognized a demand for healthy, convenient meals that cater to busy urbanites and environmentally aware individuals. Their UVP—centred on quality ingredients and sustainable practices—has helped them stand out in the competitive fast-casual space and attracted a loyal following.

2. Addressing Gaps in the Market

Competitor analysis can reveal unmet needs or gaps in the market, providing an opportunity for businesses to develop a UVP that fills those gaps. If competitors lack variety in dietary options, a new restaurant could position itself as the go-to place for vegan, gluten-free, or allergy-friendly meals, appealing to underserved customer segments.

  - Example: The Halal Guys' UVP for Halal Street Food

The Halal Guys, a New York-based food chain, found success by offering halal-certified street food in a city where demand for such options was high but supply was limited. Their UVP—serving authentic halal dishes with a New York twist—allowed them to cater to a diverse customer base seeking both authenticity and convenience. By filling a gap in the market, The Halal Guys grew from a single food cart into a successful chain with locations worldwide.

3. Incorporating Brand Personality and Story

Market research can also reveal consumer preferences for brand personalities and narratives that resonate with them. For instance, if surveys and social media analytics indicate that consumers are drawn to environmentally conscious brands, the UVP could incorporate elements of sustainability, such as eco-friendly packaging or partnerships with local farmers. Consumers today are looking for brands that not only satisfy their needs but also reflect their values, making a compelling brand story integral to a strong UVP.

  - Example: Ben & Jerry's UVP with Social Activism

Ben & Jerry's has successfully crafted a UVP that goes beyond just selling ice cream. Through their commitment to social activism and environmental sustainability, the brand appeals to consumers who value ethical business practices. Ben & Jerry's market research revealed that customers were more likely to support brands that championed social causes, and by embedding these values into their UVP, they created a strong emotional connection with their audience. This approach has differentiated Ben & Jerry's in the competitive ice cream market and attracted a loyal, values-driven customer base.

Steps to Crafting an Effective UVP Using Market Research

1. Analyse Findings from Market Research

Compile insights from surveys, focus groups, competitor analysis, and social media analytics. Look for patterns in customer preferences, gaps in competitors' offerings, and feedback on what customers value most. This data will serve as the foundation for the UVP, ensuring it is based on concrete insights rather than assumptions.

2. Identify Core Strengths and Unique Offerings

Every business has unique qualities, whether it's a signature dish, sustainable sourcing practices, or a commitment to exceptional customer service. Highlight these strengths in the UVP, focusing on those that align with the target market's needs and preferences.

3. Articulate a Clear and Compelling Statement

The UVP should be concise and specific, clearly communicating the primary reason customers should choose the business over competitors. Effective UVPs are memorable, easily understood, and resonate with the target audience's values and desires.

4. Test and Refine the UVP

Once the UVP is crafted, it can be tested with focus groups or through limited marketing campaigns. Gather feedback to determine if the UVP resonates with the intended audience and adjusts if necessary. Refining the UVP ensures it remains relevant and compelling as market trends and consumer preferences evolve.

The Power of Market Research in Shaping a Successful Food Venture

Conducting thorough market research and crafting a compelling UVP are essential steps for any culinary entrepreneur seeking to establish a successful food venture. Understanding the target market's preferences, identifying gaps in the competition, and analysing consumer feedback allow food businesses to position themselves strategically. As seen in the examples of Sweetgreen, The Halal Guys, and Ben & Jerry's, a well-defined UVP can make a brand stand out in a crowded market, attract a loyal customer base, and create lasting value.

Market research is not a one-time task but an ongoing process. Consumer preferences, trends, and competitive landscapes shift over time, and successful entrepreneurs stay attuned to these changes, continuously refining their offerings and UVP. By leveraging market research and aligning with their audience's values, culinary entrepreneurs can build brands that resonate, foster customer loyalty, and stand the test of time.

CHAPTER 5: FORMULATING A WINNING CONCEPT

In the competitive world of food ventures, having a great product isn't enough. Successful food businesses rely on a cohesive concept that goes beyond what's on the plate, encompassing theme, menu, ambiance, and brand identity. A well-formulated concept differentiates a business in a crowded market, creates memorable experiences for customers, and fosters brand loyalty. In this chapter, we will explore the essential elements of building a successful concept, from designing a cohesive theme and crafting a menu that aligns with that theme to creating an atmosphere that resonates with the target audience. We'll also analyse the success of a real-world restaurant concept that stands out in the industry.

The Foundation of a Winning Concept: Theme, Menu, and Ambiance

1. Defining the Theme

The theme of a food business serves as its overarching identity. It is the "big idea" that ties the entire concept together and gives the business its unique personality. The theme influences the menu, decor, service style, and even the type of clientele that the business attracts. Successful food businesses often select themes that reflect current trends, fill a niche, or cater to a specific audience's tastes and lifestyle preferences.

For example, a theme centred around sustainability might feature eco-friendly practices, a locally sourced menu, and minimalistic decor that evokes a sense of environmental responsibility. Alternatively, a nostalgic theme could recreate the atmosphere of a retro diner, complete with vintage furniture, a jukebox, and a menu filled with classic comfort foods.

- Aligning with Customer Expectations

It's essential that the theme aligns with the target market's values and expectations. For instance, a theme focused on health and wellness would resonate with customers who prioritize organic ingredients and balanced meals, while a theme based on fusion cuisine would appeal to adventurous diners interested in trying new and unique flavour combinations.

- Consistency Across Elements

A strong theme requires consistency across all elements of the business, from the branding and menu to the interior design and customer service style. Inconsistent themes can confuse customers and dilute the brand identity. For example, a restaurant with a rustic, farm-to-table theme would ideally have a simple, organic menu, warm lighting, natural materials, and knowledgeable staff who understand the sourcing of ingredients.

2. Crafting a Menu that Reflects the Theme

The menu is the core of any food business, and it must reflect the chosen theme in both content and presentation. A thoughtfully crafted menu complements the theme, highlights the brand's uniqueness, and caters to the preferences of the target market.

- Menu Structure and Layout

The layout of the menu itself should reinforce the theme. A high-end fine dining establishment might have an elegantly designed menu with refined descriptions, while a casual beachside café might opt for a colourful, playful menu with simple language and a relaxed tone. Visual elements like fonts, colour schemes, and illustrations should all contribute to a cohesive look that aligns with the theme.

- Signature Dishes and Unique Offerings

Signature dishes are essential in establishing a restaurant's identity. These are the dishes that embody the theme and set the restaurant apart from competitors. For instance, a tapas-style restaurant might feature small, shareable plates with unique flavour combinations, encouraging customers to try multiple items. By creating memorable, signature dishes, a restaurant gives customers a reason to return and helps build word-of-mouth marketing.

- Balancing Creativity with Customer Preferences

While creativity is important, it's equally essential to balance innovation with customer preferences. A fine line exists between offering unique dishes that stand out and creating a menu that feels too unfamiliar or inaccessible. For example, a fusion restaurant that blends Japanese and Mexican cuisine must consider how much fusion to introduce; too many unfamiliar ingredients might alienate some diners, while well-executed fusion elements can intrigue and delight customers.

3. Creating an Ambiance that Enhances the Dining Experience

Ambiance is the sensory experience of the restaurant—everything that customers see, hear, smell, and feel from the moment they enter. A successful ambiance enhances the theme and makes the dining experience immersive and enjoyable. Studies have shown that ambiance greatly influences customer satisfaction, affecting perceptions of food quality and overall experience (Kotler, 1973).

- Interior Design and Decor

The interior design should reflect the theme, creating an environment that feels authentic and inviting. A Mediterranean-inspired restaurant might use warm tones, ceramic tiles, and wooden furniture to create a relaxed, beach-like atmosphere, while a modern Asian restaurant could feature minimalist decor with clean lines and bamboo accents. Small details like table settings, lighting, and wall art contribute to an atmosphere that aligns with the concept.

- Lighting and Music

Lighting and music are crucial elements of ambiance that set the mood and influence the energy of the space. Dim, soft lighting creates an intimate feel, perfect for fine dining, while bright, natural light is more suited for casual or health-focused eateries. Music should complement the theme as well; a French bistro might play classic jazz, while a retro diner might have rock 'n' roll from the 1950s.

- Customer Flow and Seating Arrangements

The layout of the restaurant, including the placement of tables, should facilitate a smooth customer flow. High-traffic areas like the entrance, bar, and restroom should be easily accessible without disrupting seated diners. The seating arrangement should match the theme, whether it's communal tables for a casual, social atmosphere or private booths for an intimate, high-end feel.

Building a Memorable Brand Identity

Creating a memorable brand identity goes beyond aesthetics; it involves crafting a personality and voice that resonates with customers. Brand identity encompasses everything from the logo, colour scheme, and slogan to the tone of marketing messages and the values communicated by the business. A strong brand identity builds customer loyalty and makes the business more recognizable.

1. Logo and Visual Elements

The logo is often the first impression of a brand and should visually represent the restaurant's concept. A successful logo is simple, memorable, and versatile enough to be used across different media. For example, the logo for a farm-to-table restaurant might incorporate earthy colours and natural motifs, reflecting the restaurant's connection to nature and sustainability.

2. Brand Voice and Messaging

The tone of voice in marketing materials—whether playful, sophisticated, or down-to-earth—should reflect the restaurant's identity. For example, if a restaurant's theme is centred around fun, casual dining, the brand voice might be light-hearted and humorous. Brand messaging also communicates the values of the restaurant; for example, a restaurant focused on sustainability might emphasize ethical sourcing and environmental responsibility in its promotions.

3. Online Presence and Customer Engagement

In today's digital age, a restaurant's online presence is crucial for building brand identity and engaging with customers. A visually appealing and user-friendly website, active social media profiles, and positive online reviews all contribute to a strong brand presence. Social media platforms provide opportunities to share behind-the-scenes content, highlight seasonal dishes, and engage directly with customers, building a loyal online community.

- Example: The Digital Branding of Chipotle Mexican Grill

Chipotle's branding emphasizes simplicity, quality, and transparency, both in its food and its message. The brand's straightforward logo, minimalist design, and consistent focus on "Food with Integrity" resonate with customers who value fresh, responsibly sourced ingredients. Chipotle's brand voice is approachable and informative, and its social media presence often highlights the ingredients and people behind its dishes. By staying true to its brand values, Chipotle has cultivated a loyal following that appreciates both the food and the ethos of the brand.

Case Study: The Success of Noma's Concept

Noma, a restaurant based in Copenhagen, Denmark, has become an iconic name in the world of fine dining, known for its unique concept of "New Nordic Cuisine." Founded by chef René Redzepi, Noma has earned international acclaim for its dedication to local, seasonal ingredients and innovative culinary techniques. Noma's success exemplifies how a cohesive theme, meticulously crafted menu, and immersive ambiance can create a restaurant concept that stands out globally.

1. A Revolutionary Theme: New Nordic Cuisine

Noma's theme is deeply rooted in Nordic culture, emphasizing foraging, sustainability, and seasonal ingredients. Redzepi's commitment to using only local, Nordic ingredients was revolutionary at the time of Noma's inception, challenging traditional fine dining by focusing on simplicity and purity rather than luxury ingredients from around the world. This dedication to regionalism not only differentiated Noma from other fine-dining establishments but also resonated with the growing global interest in sustainability and locality.

2. Crafting a Menu that Reflects Place and Season

Noma's menu changes with the seasons, featuring dishes that highlight ingredients at their peak freshness. In spring, the menu might include wild herbs, flowers, and fresh vegetables, while winter dishes incorporate preserved items, root vegetables, and fermented products. Signature dishes, such as their famous "beetroot and plum" creation, showcase Noma's innovative approach to combining foraged ingredients with modern techniques. This seasonally driven menu not only reflects the New Nordic theme but also ensures a unique dining experience that changes throughout the year.

3. An Ambiance that Complements the Concept

The interior of Noma is minimalist yet warm, featuring natural wood, stone, and earthy colours that mirror the Nordic landscape. The dining room is designed to feel both elegant and relaxed, inviting guests to connect with the surrounding environment. Every element, from the simple table settings to the natural lighting, reinforces the theme of New Nordic Cuisine, creating an atmosphere that feels in harmony with the food.

4. Building a Global Brand from a Local Concept

Despite its local focus, Noma's concept has resonated worldwide, inspiring a movement toward local and sustainable cuisine. Through its success, Noma has become a brand synonymous with innovation, regionalism, and environmental consciousness. Redzepi's commitment to the principles of New Nordic Cuisine has made Noma an internationally recognized name, proving that a well-executed concept can transcend geographical boundaries and become a global phenomenon.

Steps to Formulating a Winning Concept for Your Own Venture

1. Identify Your Vision and Values

Begin by clarifying your vision for the restaurant and the values that will guide your brand. Consider the type of experience you want to create, the audience you aim to attract, and the unique qualities that will define your business.

2. Research and Refine Your Theme

Conduct market research to understand your target audience's preferences and identify a theme that will resonate with them. Draw inspiration from cultural trends, personal experiences, or global cuisines, but ensure the theme feels authentic and relevant.

3. Craft a Menu that Embodies the Theme

Develop a menu that aligns with your theme, featuring signature dishes that reflect the restaurant's identity. Test the menu with focus groups or pop-up events to refine the offerings based on customer feedback.

4. Design an Ambiance that Complements the Experience

Plan the interior design, lighting, music, and layout to create an ambience that enhances the theme. Pay attention to details, from the colour scheme to table settings, as these elements contribute to the overall experience.

5. Create a Cohesive Brand Identity

Build a brand identity that reflects the theme, from the logo and colour scheme to the tone of your marketing messages. Develop an online presence that reinforces your brand and engages customers through social media and community involvement.

Bringing Your Concept to Life

A well-formulated concept is more than just a theme; it's a complete experience that resonates with customers and creates lasting memories. As seen in the success of brands like Chipotle and Noma, a cohesive theme, thoughtfully crafted menu, immersive ambience, and strong brand identity are essential components of a winning concept. By understanding these elements and applying them to their own ventures, culinary entrepreneurs can build brands that stand out, foster customer loyalty, and leave a lasting impact in the food industry.

Formulating a winning concept requires vision, creativity, and meticulous planning. When executed well, it has the power to transform a simple dining experience into something extraordinary, ensuring the business's success in a competitive market.

CHAPTER 6: BUSINESS PLAN ESSENTIALS FOR FOOD ENTREPRENEURS

Creating a successful food business requires more than just a passion for cooking and creativity in the kitchen. A detailed, well-thought-out business plan serves as the blueprint for transforming ideas into a successful venture. In a competitive industry like food service, where operational and financial demands are high, a business plan provides essential structure, ensuring that entrepreneurs consider every aspect of their business before launch. This chapter will examine the key components of a solid business plan, explain how a business plan acts as a roadmap for success, and provide a real-world example of a comprehensive food business plan.

The Role of a Business Plan as a Roadmap

A business plan is a strategic document that outlines the goals, target market, operational structure, financial projections, and competitive strategy of a business. For food entrepreneurs, it acts as both a planning tool and a guiding framework, allowing them to make informed decisions, track progress, and adapt as the business evolves.

A well-prepared business plan offers several benefits:

- Guides Operational Strategy: By setting clear objectives, the plan provides direction for each stage of the business's development, from sourcing ingredients and selecting a location to hiring staff and setting pricing strategies.
- Attracts Investors and Lenders: Investors and lenders require a solid business plan to assess the viability and profitability of the venture before providing funding. A detailed financial projection and market analysis demonstrate that the entrepreneur understands the business environment and potential challenges.
- Helps in Goal Setting and Performance Tracking: A business plan includes measurable goals, allowing entrepreneurs to track their progress, adjust strategies as needed, and stay on course to achieve their objectives.
- Supports Decision-Making: From pricing and menu design to marketing and growth strategies, a business plan helps entrepreneurs make informed decisions aligned with their overall vision.

As the foundation of a food business, a business plan

provides the stability and direction needed to achieve sustainable growth in a competitive market.

Key Components of a Solid Business Plan for Food Entrepreneurs

1. Executive Summary

The executive summary is the first section of a business plan and provides a high-level overview of the business. It includes the business's name, location, concept, target market, and mission statement. The executive summary should be concise yet compelling, capturing the essence of the business and its potential for success. Investors and lenders often rely on the executive summary to decide whether to read further, so it's essential to make a strong first impression.

- Example: For a food truck business focused on healthy, sustainable cuisine, the executive summary might state:

"Green Bites is a sustainable, plant-based food truck concept based in Austin, Texas, dedicated to providing convenient, delicious, and eco-friendly meals. Targeting health-conscious millennials and environmentally aware consumers, Green Bites offers a seasonal menu sourced from local farms and served in compostable packaging. Our mission is to promote healthy eating and environmental responsibility, making sustainable dining accessible and enjoyable."

2. Mission Statement

The mission statement outlines the business's purpose, core values, and goals. For food entrepreneurs, the mission statement reflects the principles that will guide their operations, customer interactions, and brand messaging. A strong mission statement creates a sense of purpose for the business and resonates with customers who share similar values.

- Example: A mission statement for a farm-to-table restaurant might read:

"At Harvest & Hearth, our mission is to deliver an authentic, seasonal dining experience that celebrates local farms and sustainable practices. We believe in using fresh, responsibly sourced ingredients to craft dishes that nourish both our community and the environment."

3. Market Analysis

Market analysis is a critical component of a business plan, as it provides insights into the industry, target market, and competitive landscape. It involves researching the demographics, preferences, and behaviours of the intended customer base, as well as evaluating competitors' strengths and weaknesses. For food entrepreneurs, understanding market demand, consumer trends, and competitor offerings is essential for positioning their business effectively.

- Industry Overview: Briefly outline the current state of the food industry, including trends like health consciousness, convenience, or eco-friendliness, as applicable to the business.

- Target Market Analysis: Describe the characteristics of the target audience, including age, income level, lifestyle, dining preferences, and spending habits.

- Competitive Analysis: Identify key competitors in the area, analysing their menu, pricing, location, and customer reviews. Highlight any gaps in the market that the business can fill.

- Example: For a vegan café targeting a millennial demographic in Los Angeles, the market analysis might reveal high demand for plant-based dining options. The analysis would show that while there are several vegan establishments, few focus on affordable, grab-and-go options, creating an opportunity to attract budget-conscious, health-focused consumers.

4. Product and Menu Offerings

This section details the primary products or menu items the business will offer, aligning them with the theme and target market. For food businesses, the menu is central to the brand's identity, so this section should showcase the unique features and benefits of each offering, highlighting any signature dishes or seasonal items.

- Menu Description: Include a sample menu with descriptions of key items. Explain how each dish aligns with the brand concept and appeals to the target market.
- Sourcing and Ingredients: Describe sourcing practices, especially if the business focuses on locally grown or organic ingredients. Sustainable or specialty sourcing can be a valuable aspect of the brand's appeal.
- Example: For a Mediterranean-inspired fast-casual restaurant, the menu might include items like falafel bowls, pita wraps, and mezze platters, with an emphasis on fresh vegetables, whole grains, and house-made sauces. Highlighting the use of locally sourced ingredients can enhance the menu's appeal to health-conscious diners.

5. Operations Plan

The operations plan outlines the logistics of running the business, from day-to-day management to staffing and supplier relationships. This section is particularly important for food businesses, where efficient operations directly impact product quality and customer satisfaction.

- Location and Facility Requirements: Describe the type of space needed, such as a commercial kitchen for a catering business or a food truck with specific cooking equipment.
- Staffing: Outline the roles required, including chefs, servers, cashiers, and other team members. Include a plan for hiring, training, and managing staff.
- Suppliers and Vendors: Identify reliable suppliers for ingredients, packaging, and equipment. Establishing strong relationships with suppliers is crucial for ensuring consistency and quality.
- Operational Workflow: Provide an overview of daily processes, including inventory management, food preparation, quality control, and waste reduction practices.

- Example: For a bakery, the operations plan would cover key aspects such as sourcing flour from local mills, employing skilled pastry chefs, and maintaining a clean and organized kitchen. Daily workflow might involve early morning baking, continuous product restocking, and meticulous inventory tracking.

6. Marketing and Sales Strategy

The marketing and sales strategy describes how the

business will attract and retain customers. For food entrepreneurs, a strong marketing strategy is essential for building brand awareness, driving foot traffic, and encouraging repeat business. This section should cover both online and offline marketing tactics, such as social media, local partnerships, and customer loyalty programs.

- Brand Positioning: Define how the business will be positioned in the market, highlighting its unique value proposition.
- Marketing Channels: Identify the platforms that will be used for promotion, such as Instagram, Facebook, Yelp, or local food blogs.
- Customer Engagement and Retention: Explain how the business will build relationships with customers through loyalty programs, community events, or special promotions.

- Example: A smoothie and juice bar targeting health-conscious millennials might use Instagram for visual storytelling, posting vibrant images of freshly made juices and featuring customer testimonials. A loyalty program offering discounts for frequent visits can encourage customer retention.

7. Financial Projections

Financial projections provide a forecast of expected revenue, expenses, and profits. This section is vital for demonstrating the business's financial viability to potential investors or lenders. Typical components include startup costs, operating expenses, projected sales, and cash flow projections.

- Startup Costs: Estimate initial expenses, such as equipment, renovations, licenses, and marketing.
- Revenue Projections: Forecast monthly and annual revenue based on market demand and pricing strategy.
- Break-even Analysis: Calculate the point at which the business's revenue covers all expenses.
- Profit and Loss Statement: Project the business's net income over the first three years.

- Example: For a small coffee shop, startup costs might include furniture, espresso machines, interior decor, and initial inventory. Monthly revenue projections could be based on estimated customer traffic and average spending per visit. Financial projections should be realistic and backed by market research, showing a clear path to profitability.

Real-World Example: A Sample Business Plan for "Green Spoon Café"

Business Concept:
Green Spoon Café is a fast-casual, eco-friendly café located in Portland, Oregon. The café specializes in organic, locally sourced plant-based dishes, catering to health-conscious millennials and environmentally aware consumers. With a cozy, rustic ambiance, Green Spoon Café combines sustainable dining with convenience, offering both dine-in and takeout options.

Executive Summary:
Green Spoon Café's mission is to provide nutritious, delicious, and eco-friendly meals that support local farmers and promote sustainability. Our target market

consists of young professionals and families in Portland who prioritize health and environmental responsibility. With an accessible price point and a unique blend of flavours, Green Spoon Café aims to redefine plant-based dining in the local community.

Market Analysis:
Portland has a high demand for eco-friendly and health-conscious dining options. Market research shows that 62% of Portland residents prefer organic ingredients, and 78% of millennials express willingness to pay more for sustainable food. Despite a growing number of plant-based eateries, few offer affordable, fast-casual options, making Green Spoon Café well-positioned to fill this gap.

Product and Menu Offerings:
Green Spoon Café's menu includes items such as Buddha bowls, grain-based salads, smoothie bowls, and homemade dressings. Signature dishes include the "Green Goodness Bowl" and the "Turmeric-Infused Cauliflower Wrap," highlighting local produce and nutrient-dense ingredients. All packaging is compostable, aligning with the café's eco-friendly mission.

Operations Plan:
Located in downtown Portland, Green Spoon Café will operate from 8 AM to 8 PM daily. The team includes a head chef, sous chef, line cooks, and front-of-house staff trained in sustainable practices. Ingredients will be sourced from local farms, and a commercial composter will manage food waste to reduce environmental impact.

Marketing and Sales Strategy:
Green Spoon Café will use Instagram and Facebook

to showcase menu items and engage with customers. Partnerships with local fitness studios and health food stores will further strengthen the brand's visibility. Monthly events like "Sustainability Sundays" will invite the community to learn about eco-friendly practices, fostering customer loyalty and brand awareness.

Financial Projections:
Startup costs for Green Spoon Café are estimated at $120,000, covering kitchen equipment, renovations, and initial inventory. Monthly revenue is projected at $25,000, with an anticipated break-even point within the first 18 months. Annual revenue is forecasted to grow by 15% as brand recognition increases.

Crafting a Blueprint for Success

A comprehensive business plan is the cornerstone of a successful food venture. By laying out every aspect of the business, from mission and target market to financial forecasts and operational details, entrepreneurs create a roadmap that guides them toward their goals. As illustrated in the sample business plan for Green Spoon Café, a well-defined plan provides clarity, attracts investors, and equips entrepreneurs with the tools needed to make informed decisions.

For food entrepreneurs, the business plan is more than just a formality—it's a strategic document that transforms vision into reality. With a clear plan in place, culinary entrepreneurs are better positioned to build sustainable, successful, and memorable food businesses.

CHAPTER 7: FUNDING YOUR CULINARY VENTURE

Starting a food business, whether it's a restaurant, food truck, or catering service, requires a significant financial investment. From securing a location to purchasing equipment and ingredients, the costs associated with launching a culinary venture can be substantial. Finding the right funding sources is crucial for setting up a solid foundation for the business and ensuring it has the resources needed to succeed. In this chapter, we'll explore various funding options available to culinary entrepreneurs, discuss the pros and cons of each method, and examine real-world success stories of food businesses that leveraged alternative funding sources to bring their concepts to life.

Options for Financing a Culinary Venture

1. Personal Savings

Many food entrepreneurs start by using their personal savings to fund their business. This option can be advantageous as it allows the owner to retain full control and equity without the need to repay loans or answer to investors. However, using personal savings carries risks, especially if the business doesn't generate revenue as quickly as expected. It's essential to assess one's financial stability before committing significant personal funds to a new venture.

- Advantages: Complete control over the business, no debt obligations, no need to share profits or equity.

- Disadvantages: High personal financial risk, limited access to additional capital, potential impact on personal financial stability.

- Example: Ina Garten's Barefoot Contessa

When Ina Garten purchased a specialty food store in the Hamptons in 1978, she used her personal savings to fund the acquisition. Starting small and focusing on high-quality ingredients, Garten gradually built the brand. By reinvesting profits back into the business, she was able to expand without external funding. Today, Barefoot Contessa has become a successful brand, demonstrating how personal savings can provide the foundation for a sustainable business if managed prudently.

2. Small Business Loans

Small business loans are one of the most common financing methods for culinary entrepreneurs. Loans can be secured through traditional banks or specialized lenders that work with small businesses. The Small

Business Administration (SBA) in the United States, for example, offers various loan programs designed to support entrepreneurs, including low-interest loans for startups. However, small business loans require a solid credit score, a well-prepared business plan, and may necessitate collateral.

- Advantages: Access to a substantial amount of capital, predictable repayment structure, no dilution of ownership.
- Disadvantages: Debt obligations with interest, possible requirement for collateral, potential difficulty in securing approval for new businesses without credit history.

- Example: Sweetgreen's Initial Funding

Sweetgreen, a popular fast-casual salad chain, initially used a small business loan to fund their first location in Georgetown. Founders Jonathan Neman, Nicolas Jammet, and Nathaniel Ru saw an opportunity to cater to health-conscious customers with a farm-to-table approach but needed capital to bring their concept to life. With a strong business plan and commitment to quality, Sweetgreen secured the loan, leading to its successful launch and eventual expansion into a nationwide brand.

3. Investors

Investors provide capital in exchange for equity in the business. For food entrepreneurs, this can mean working with angel investors, venture capitalists, or even friends and family. Investors bring not only funding but often business expertise and industry connections that can be valuable for growth. However, giving up equity means sharing ownership and, potentially, some control over the business.

- Advantages: Access to large sums of capital, potential guidance and mentorship from experienced investors, no debt obligations.

- Disadvantages: Loss of full ownership, potential conflicts with investors over business direction, requirement to share profits.

- Example: Shake Shack's Expansion with Venture Capital

After Shake Shack's initial success, the brand attracted attention from venture capitalists who saw the potential for nationwide growth. The investment allowed Shake Shack to open new locations, refine its branding, and scale operations. Partnering with investors provided Shake Shack with the resources and expertise needed to become one of the most recognized fast-casual brands in the United States. This example illustrates how strategic investment can help a food business expand significantly beyond its initial location.

4. Crowdfunding

Crowdfunding has become an increasingly popular method for food entrepreneurs seeking to fund their ventures without traditional loans or investors. Platforms like Kickstarter, Indiegogo, and GoFundMe allow entrepreneurs to raise funds from individuals who believe in their concept. Crowdfunding works by offering backers rewards, such as free meals, merchandise, or exclusive experiences, in exchange for their support. Crowdfunding campaigns often serve as valuable marketing tools, creating early buzz and building a loyal customer base even before the business launches.

- Advantages: Low risk, opportunity to gauge public interest, no debt or loss of equity, early marketing and brand visibility.

- Disadvantages: Unpredictable results, campaign management can be time-consuming, funds may fall short of the required amount.

- Example: Broth Lab's Successful Kickstarter Campaign

Broth Lab, a specialty broth company, turned to Kickstarter to raise funds for its initial product line. By showcasing the quality of their broth and emphasizing their commitment to locally sourced ingredients, they attracted a community of backers who shared their passion for healthy, sustainable food. Broth Lab exceeded its funding goal, enabling the founders to establish production and distribution channels. The campaign also helped build an initial customer base, as backers became some of Broth Lab's most loyal advocates.

5. Grants and Contests

Grants and contests offer funding opportunities that do not require repayment or equity exchange. Some organizations, government programs, and industry groups provide grants specifically for small food businesses, such as those focusing on sustainability, community impact, or culinary innovation. Contests, such as pitch competitions for startups, also offer a way to win seed funding, although these are often highly competitive.

- Advantages: No repayment or loss of equity, prestige and visibility from winning contests, potential networking opportunities.

- Disadvantages: Highly competitive, limited funding amounts, time-consuming application process.

  - Example: The Halcyon Incubator and Soupergirl
  Soupergirl, a Washington, D.C.-based company offering plant-based soups, received support through the Halcyon Incubator, a program that provides funding, mentorship, and resources for socially conscious businesses. This support allowed Soupergirl to expand production, refine branding, and enhance its distribution network. Founder Sara Polon leveraged the resources from Halcyon to grow Soupergirl into a successful and sustainable business that aligns with her mission of promoting healthy, plant-based eating.

Strategic Use of Funds

Regardless of the funding source, managing capital effectively is essential. Allocating funds strategically can help food businesses operate smoothly, grow sustainably, and maintain financial health. Here are key areas where culinary entrepreneurs should prioritize spending:

1. Startup Costs: Covering one-time expenses such as kitchen equipment, renovations, licenses, and branding.
2. Inventory and Ingredients: Ensuring a consistent supply of quality ingredients is critical, especially for businesses focusing on freshness and sustainability.
3. Marketing and Brand Development: Building brand awareness through social media, advertising, and community events to attract a loyal customer base.
4. Operating Expenses: Managing monthly costs, including rent, utilities, payroll, and insurance, to ensure

steady operations.

5. Buffer for Unforeseen Costs: Setting aside funds for unexpected expenses, such as equipment repairs, seasonal downturns, or regulatory changes, provides financial stability.

Success Stories of Food Businesses Using Alternative Funding Sources

1. Junzi Kitchen and Angel Investors

Founded by a group of Yale graduates, Junzi Kitchen offers a modern take on northern Chinese cuisine. Initially, the founders reached out to angel investors who shared their vision of introducing authentic yet accessible Chinese food to an American audience. Angel investors provided Junzi Kitchen with the capital needed to open their first location in New Haven, Connecticut. The funding allowed Junzi Kitchen to invest in quality ingredients, interior design, and branding, which played a pivotal role in establishing their concept. With the support of these early investors, Junzi Kitchen has since expanded to multiple locations and continues to grow.

2. Compton Vegan's Crowdfunding Success

Compton Vegan, a plant-based soul food business founded by Lemel Durrah in Compton, California, leveraged crowdfunding to gain visibility and funding for his business. By sharing his story and mission of making plant-based eating accessible in underserved communities, Durrah's GoFundMe campaign resonated

with backers. The funds raised allowed Compton Vegan to expand operations and serve a larger customer base.

Durrah's journey demonstrates how crowdfunding can provide essential startup capital while fostering a loyal community of supporters.

3. KIND Snacks' Bootstrapped Beginnings

KIND Snacks, founded by Daniel Lubetzky, is a prime example of a business that initially relied on personal savings and bootstrapping. Lubetzky launched KIND with the vision of creating a healthier snack option, using his savings to fund product development and marketing. Although he faced financial challenges in the early stages, Lubetzky's commitment to quality and brand messaging eventually led to significant growth. Today, KIND Snacks is a multimillion-dollar brand, proving that self-funding and disciplined financial management can drive long-term success.

Choosing the Right Funding Path for Your Culinary Venture

Funding a food business is a crucial step in bringing an entrepreneurial vision to life. Each funding option—whether it's personal savings, small business loans, investors, crowdfunding, or grants—offers unique benefits and challenges. The right choice depends on the entrepreneur's financial situation, business goals, and willingness to share ownership or take on debt.

As seen in the success stories of brands like Junzi Kitchen, Compton Vegan, and KIND Snacks, a strategic approach to funding can help culinary entrepreneurs build a strong foundation, achieve sustainable growth, and ultimately realize their vision. By selecting the most suitable financing option and using funds wisely, food entrepreneurs can navigate the financial complexities of the industry and position their businesses for lasting success.

CHAPTER 8: FINANCIAL PLANNING AND BUDGETING

Effective financial planning is the backbone of any successful food business. From restaurants to food trucks, culinary ventures face unique financial demands due to high initial investments, operational costs, and often narrow profit margins. Without proper financial planning, many food businesses struggle to maintain cash flow, cover expenses, and sustain growth over the long term. This chapter delves into the core components of financial planning and budgeting in the food industry, covering essentials like cash flow management, break-even analysis, pricing strategies, cost control, and financial forecasting.

Understanding the Basics: Cash Flow, Budgeting, and Break-Even Analysis

1. Cash Flow Management

Cash flow refers to the movement of money in and out of a business, and for food entrepreneurs, maintaining positive cash flow is essential for covering daily expenses and handling unexpected costs. Cash flow management involves tracking income from sales, controlling expenses, and ensuring there is enough cash on hand to sustain operations.

- Operating Cash Flow: This is the cash generated from daily operations, including sales revenue from food and beverages. Managing operating cash flow helps ensure that the business has sufficient funds to pay for essentials like ingredients, wages, and utilities.

- Cash Flow Challenges in the Food Industry: Many food businesses face cash flow challenges due to seasonal demand, fluctuating ingredient costs, and potential delays in payments. For instance, a restaurant may experience lower cash flow in winter but higher expenses for heating, making cash flow management especially critical during slower periods.

- Example: To address cash flow variability, many cafes and bakeries offer seasonal promotions or pre-orders for holiday treats to increase sales during off-peak months. Strategies like these help maintain steady income even when customer foot traffic is low.

2. Budgeting Essentials

Budgeting involves creating a financial plan that outlines projected expenses and revenue over a specified period. In the food industry, budgeting helps entrepreneurs anticipate costs, allocate funds strategically, and avoid overspending. A well-prepared budget includes categories such as labour costs, food and beverage expenses, rent, marketing, and miscellaneous operational costs.

- Setting a Realistic Budget: To create an accurate budget, entrepreneurs should assess both fixed and variable costs. Fixed costs, like rent and salaries, remain relatively constant, while variable costs, such as ingredients and utilities, fluctuate based on demand and seasonality.

- Regular Review and Adjustment: Food businesses operate in a dynamic environment, where changes in ingredient prices or labour rates can impact the budget. Regularly reviewing and adjusting the budget ensures that the business remains aligned with financial goals and adapts to unforeseen changes.

- Example: A catering business might set a monthly budget for food purchases based on client bookings. However, if ingredient prices rise due to supply chain disruptions, adjusting the budget can prevent overspending and preserve profit margins.

3. Break-Even Analysis

Break-even analysis is a financial tool that calculates the point at which a business's revenue equals its expenses, resulting in neither profit nor loss. For food entrepreneurs, this analysis is crucial for understanding how much sales revenue is needed to cover all operational costs.

- Calculating Break-Even Point: To determine the break-even point, divide fixed costs by the contribution margin per unit (price per dish minus variable costs per dish).

This calculation shows the number of units or sales required to cover costs.

- Importance of Break-Even Analysis: Conducting a break-even analysis helps food businesses set realistic revenue goals, understand minimum sales targets, and make informed decisions about menu pricing and portion sizes.

- Example: A food truck with $5,000 in monthly fixed costs and a $2 contribution margin per item would need to sell 2,500 items per month to break even. This insight allows the owner to set daily sales targets and plan for profitable growth.

Pricing Strategies and Controlling Operational Costs

1. Effective Pricing Strategies

Pricing is a critical component of financial planning in the food industry. The right pricing strategy helps cover costs, appeal to the target market, and generate profit, but setting prices involves more than simply marking up costs. Successful pricing strategies take customer demand, competitor pricing, and perceived value into account.

- Cost-Plus Pricing: This straightforward approach involves adding a markup to the cost of ingredients to determine the selling price. While simple to implement, it may not fully capture the value perceived by customers or market conditions.
- Value-Based Pricing: In value-based pricing, prices are set based on customers' perceived value of the product. This approach works well for restaurants that

offer unique dining experiences, premium ingredients, or specialty dishes that differentiate them from competitors.

- Competitive Pricing: This strategy involves setting prices based on competitors' prices for similar offerings. While this can attract cost-conscious customers, it may not be sustainable if competitor prices are lower than the business's cost structure allows.

- Example: A fine dining restaurant may use value-based pricing for its signature dishes, charging a premium that reflects the exclusive ambiance, culinary expertise, and high-quality ingredients. On the other hand, a food truck may adopt competitive pricing to attract price-sensitive customers at popular festivals.

2. Controlling Operational Costs

Managing operational costs is essential for maximizing profitability. In the food industry, primary cost areas include labour, food and beverage, rent, and utilities. By controlling these costs, food businesses can improve their bottom line without compromising quality or customer experience.

- Labor Cost Management: Labor is often one of the largest expenses for food businesses. Optimizing staff schedules, cross-training employees, and reducing overtime can help control labour costs. Some restaurants use scheduling software to forecast staffing needs based on expected sales and peak hours.

- Reducing Food Waste: Food waste contributes to unnecessary expenses and reduces profitability. Implementing portion control, using inventory management systems, and creating specials to use surplus ingredients are effective ways to minimize waste.

- Energy Efficiency: Reducing utility costs is another way to manage expenses. Energy-efficient equipment, LED lighting, and regular maintenance can help decrease electricity and gas bills over time.

- Example: A small restaurant might adopt a "nose-to-tail" approach, using every part of an ingredient to reduce waste. For instance, leftover vegetable scraps can be used to make broth, while offcuts of meat can be incorporated into soups or stews. This approach reduces waste, controls food costs, and creates additional menu items.

The Importance of Financial Forecasting for Long-Term Sustainability

Financial forecasting is the process of estimating future revenue, expenses, and profits based on historical data and market trends. For food businesses, accurate forecasting is essential for strategic planning, budgeting, and securing funding from investors or lenders. Financial forecasting also helps entrepreneurs prepare for seasonal fluctuations, market shifts, and economic uncertainties.

1. Types of Financial Forecasting

   - Sales Forecasting: Projecting sales based on past performance, customer demand, and marketing efforts. Sales forecasts help determine inventory needs, staffing requirements, and promotional timing.
   - Expense Forecasting: Estimating future expenses, including fixed and variable costs. Accurate expense forecasts allow businesses to budget effectively and

ensure they have enough funds to cover upcoming costs.

- Cash Flow Forecasting: Predicting future cash inflows and outflows to maintain positive cash flow. Cash flow forecasts are crucial for planning large purchases, managing debt repayment, and handling potential shortfalls.

- Example: A seasonal ice cream shop might forecast increased sales during the summer months and lower sales in winter. By forecasting cash flow accurately, the shop can plan for off-season expenses and implement promotions or temporary winter menu items to maintain revenue.

2. Developing an Actionable Financial Plan

Financial forecasting should be integrated into a broader financial plan that outlines strategies for achieving the business's financial goals. An actionable financial plan includes monthly, quarterly, and annual projections, along with contingency plans to address potential challenges.

- Setting Financial Milestones: Establishing specific financial milestones, such as reaching a certain revenue target or reducing food costs by a set percentage, helps entrepreneurs stay on track and measure progress.

- Adapting to Changes: Financial forecasts should be flexible enough to adapt to changes in the market, such as shifts in consumer demand, ingredient costs, or regulatory requirements. Regularly reviewing and adjusting the forecast ensures it remains relevant and reflective of current conditions.

- Example: A fast-casual chain might set a milestone

to achieve a 10% profit margin by the end of its second year. If the forecast indicates that ingredient costs are higher than expected, the chain can adjust menu prices, renegotiate with suppliers, or explore alternative ingredients to meet its profit goal.

Case Study: Financial Planning for "Herb & Spice Café"

Herb & Spice Café is a plant-based restaurant in Denver, Colorado, focusing on seasonal, locally sourced ingredients. Here's an example of how Herb & Spice Café might approach financial planning and budgeting to achieve sustainable growth:

1. Cash Flow Management:

Herb & Spice Café experiences fluctuating cash flow due to Denver's seasonal tourist traffic. To address this, the café maintains a cash reserve from high summer earnings to cover winter expenses. They also offer seasonal promotions, such as holiday meal kits in December, to boost off-peak sales.

2. Budgeting:

The café sets an annual budget that includes monthly allocations for food costs, labour, rent, marketing, and utilities. The budget accounts for variable costs, such as seasonal produce, by allowing a flexible spending range. Management reviews the budget monthly to identify cost-saving opportunities and adjust for unexpected expenses.

3. Break-Even Analysis:

Herb & Spice Café's break-even analysis reveals that it must generate $40,000 in monthly revenue to cover fixed and variable costs. Knowing this target,

the café sets weekly sales goals and uses daily reports to track progress. When sales fall short, they implement special promotions to attract more customers.

4. Pricing Strategy:

The café uses value-based pricing for its premium dishes, like the "Seasonal Tasting Plate," which showcases limited-time ingredients. For staple menu items, Herb & Spice Café employs cost-plus pricing to ensure affordability while covering ingredient costs and achieving a 30% markup.

5. Financial Forecasting and Planning:

Herb & Spice Café prepares quarterly financial forecasts, factoring in expected sales growth and anticipated expenses. Their forecast for 2023 includes an increase in ingredient costs due to inflation. To maintain profit margins, they plan to adjust menu prices by 5% and introduce a "chef's choice" seasonal menu to encourage customers to try high-margin items.

Building a Financially Sound Food Business

Financial planning and budgeting are indispensable for achieving success in the food industry. By effectively managing cash flow, setting realistic budgets, conducting break-even analyses, and establishing smart pricing strategies, culinary entrepreneurs can maintain a healthy financial foundation. Financial forecasting further supports sustainability, enabling businesses to anticipate changes, prepare for seasonal fluctuations, and set achievable financial goals.

As demonstrated in the Herb & Spice Café case study, strategic financial planning helps food businesses control costs, maximize profits, and ensure long-term viability. With a solid financial plan in place, entrepreneurs are better equipped to make informed decisions that drive growth, adapt to challenges, and navigate the complexities of the food industry.

CHAPTER 9: NAVIGATING LEGAL AND REGULATORY REQUIREMENTS

Starting and running a food business requires more than culinary skills and a strong business plan; it also demands thorough knowledge of legal and regulatory requirements. Compliance with these regulations ensures the safety of customers, protects employees, and keeps the business in good standing with authorities. Navigating the legal landscape can be challenging, especially as laws vary by location and may be subject to frequent updates. This chapter will outline essential licenses, permits, and food safety regulations for food businesses, discuss compliance with health codes, employee laws, and zoning ordinances, and provide real-life examples of challenges and solutions in legal compliance.

Essential Licenses and Permits for Food Businesses

To legally operate a food business, entrepreneurs must obtain various licenses and permits that vary depending on the type of business and location. Understanding the required paperwork and submitting applications on time are crucial steps in the startup process.

1. Business License

A business license grants permission to operate within a specific jurisdiction, whether it's a city, county, or state. This is one of the first permits a food business needs, as it legally allows the establishment to conduct business.

- Application Process: Typically, entrepreneurs apply through the local city or county clerk's office. Requirements and fees vary, but most applications require business details, a description of activities, and payment of a licensing fee.
- Renewal: Business licenses often need annual renewal, with some municipalities requiring additional inspections for food businesses to ensure compliance.

2. Food Handler's Permit and Food Manager Certification

Food handler's permits are generally required for all employees who handle food, while food manager certification is often mandatory for at least one person on staff, such as the head chef or kitchen manager. These certifications confirm that employees understand basic food safety practices.

- Training and Testing: Food handler permits usually involve a short training session and a test on topics like food handling, hygiene, and temperature control. Food manager certifications are more extensive, covering advanced topics in food safety and kitchen management.

- Example: In California, food handlers must complete a food handler training course and pass an examination, while restaurant managers require a Food Protection Manager Certification.

3. Health Department Permit

Health permits, often known as food establishment permits, are required for any business that prepares, stores, or serves food to the public. The local health department inspects the establishment to ensure it meets sanitary and safety standards.

- Inspection Process: Health department inspectors check food storage, preparation areas, equipment, and cleanliness. They may also evaluate employee hygiene practices, pest control measures, and waste management.

- Reinspections: Health departments may conduct periodic reinspections to verify ongoing compliance with health codes. Failure to pass can lead to fines or even closure.

- Example: Health inspectors closed a restaurant in New York City after finding repeated violations, including inadequate refrigeration and improper food storage. The owner implemented new sanitation protocols, conducted staff training, and passed a reinspection, allowing the restaurant to reopen.

4. Liquor License

If a restaurant or bar intends to serve alcohol, it must obtain a liquor license. These permits are heavily regulated, and the application process can be lengthy and complex, often involving background checks and local zoning considerations.

- Types of Liquor Licenses: Many states offer different licenses based on the type of alcohol served (e.g., beer and wine only, full liquor) and whether the alcohol is consumed on-site or sold for off-site consumption.
- Application Process: Applicants usually apply through a state liquor authority, which may include public hearings, neighbourhood input, and strict conditions on the sale and serving of alcohol.

- Example: In Boston, a restaurant faced delays in obtaining a liquor license due to community opposition. After holding meetings with local residents and agreeing to limited hours, the business secured the license and was able to open.

5. Sign Permit

Sign permits are required in many municipalities to control the appearance and size of business signage, maintaining local aesthetics and safety. The rules vary widely, with some areas imposing strict limits on size, height, lighting, and placement.

- Application Process: Businesses submit a design proposal that often includes dimensions, materials, and location. Some jurisdictions require approval from planning committees or neighbourhood associations.
- Example: A bakery in San Francisco had to alter its original signage design after city regulators raised concerns about its size. By adjusting the design to meet local guidelines, the bakery obtained approval and

installed its sign.

Compliance with Health Codes, Employee Laws, and Zoning Ordinances

1. Health Code Compliance

Health codes exist to protect public health by ensuring that food establishments maintain high standards of cleanliness and hygiene. These regulations cover food storage, preparation, sanitation, temperature control, pest management, and more.

- Regular Inspections: Health departments conduct routine inspections to verify compliance. Common violations include improper food storage, failure to sanitize surfaces, and inadequate handwashing facilities.
- Employee Training: Educating employees on proper hygiene, cross-contamination prevention, and correct food handling practices reduces the risk of violations and promotes a safe dining environment.

- Example: A restaurant in Chicago failed an inspection due to improperly stored raw meat, which risked cross-contamination. To remedy the issue, the management implemented a new storage system, conducted staff training on food safety, and passed the next inspection.

2. Employee Laws

Compliance with labour laws is essential to maintain a fair and safe work environment. Employee laws cover areas like minimum wage, overtime pay, employee rights, workplace safety, and anti-discrimination policies.

- Wages and Overtime: Food businesses must adhere to

federal and state minimum wage laws and pay employees overtime as required. Violations can lead to legal action and fines.

- Workplace Safety: Businesses are required to provide a safe environment, comply with Occupational Safety and Health Administration (OSHA) standards, and ensure that employees are trained to use equipment safely.

- Anti-Discrimination and Harassment: Federal and state laws prohibit discrimination based on factors like race, gender, religion, and disability. Businesses must also address any harassment claims promptly and establish a zero-tolerance policy.

- Example: A café in Los Angeles was fined for failing to pay proper overtime wages. Following an audit, the owner introduced a timekeeping system to accurately track hours and provided training on wage compliance.

3. Zoning Ordinances

Zoning laws regulate where certain types of businesses can operate within a city or county. For food businesses, zoning ordinances often dictate permissible locations, hours of operation, and whether the establishment can serve alcohol or provide outdoor seating.

- Zoning Types: Different zoning categories, such as commercial, residential, and mixed-use, have specific restrictions. Entrepreneurs must ensure their business location is compatible with local zoning laws.

- Conditional Use Permits: In some cases, businesses may apply for a conditional use permit to operate in an area where their type of establishment is not typically allowed. Approval depends on factors like community impact, noise levels, and traffic.

- Example: A food truck in Austin, Texas, faced zoning restrictions that limited where it could park. After collaborating with local officials and securing a permit for specific locations, the owner successfully navigated zoning challenges to maintain a profitable route.

Real-Life Examples of Challenges and Solutions in Legal Compliance

1. Food Safety Challenge: Chipotle Mexican Grill's Health Code Violations

Chipotle Mexican Grill faced major health code challenges in 2015, when several outbreaks of foodborne illness were linked to their locations. These incidents led to temporary store closures, extensive media scrutiny, and a decline in customer trust. In response, Chipotle implemented rigorous new safety measures, including high-resolution ingredient tracking, increased employee training, and independent food safety audits.

- Solution: By investing heavily in food safety improvements and employee education, Chipotle rebuilt its reputation and regained customer trust. This example underscores the importance of proactive compliance and the need for food businesses to address health issues immediately.

2. Employee Law Challenge: Shake Shack's Wage Compliance

Shake Shack, a popular fast-casual restaurant chain, encountered wage compliance issues related to tipping practices. Employees claimed they were not compensated fairly for overtime hours and tips. Following a lawsuit, Shake Shack reassessed its payroll policies and committed to ensuring fair wages and clear tip distribution practices.

- Solution: Shake Shack implemented a transparent tip-sharing policy and revised timekeeping practices to ensure all employees were paid accurately. This case highlights the importance of adhering to labour laws and maintaining fair pay practices to avoid legal complications and maintain employee morale.

3. Zoning Challenge: Seattle's "Little Big Burger" and Outdoor Seating Restrictions

Little Big Burger, a burger chain in Seattle, faced zoning challenges when it applied for outdoor seating in a mixed-use neighbourhood. Local zoning laws restricted outdoor dining in certain areas to limit noise and maintain residential quality of life. After several community meetings and a compromise with city planners, Little Big Burger obtained approval for limited outdoor seating with restricted hours.

- Solution: The business worked with local officials and nearby residents to address concerns, demonstrating how food businesses can navigate zoning restrictions by fostering positive community relationships.

Practical Steps for Navigating Legal Compliance

1. Research and Understand Local Regulations

Each city, county, and state has its own set of regulations. Entrepreneurs should research and understand the requirements for their specific location, including health codes, labour laws, and zoning ordinances.

2. Consult Legal Professionals

Consulting with legal professionals or regulatory consultants who specialize in the food industry can provide valuable guidance and ensure the business complies with complex regulations.

3. Develop a Compliance Checklist

A checklist of required licenses, permits, and health standards helps streamline

the compliance process. Regularly reviewing the checklist and updating it as regulations change ensures ongoing adherence.

4. Train Employees on Compliance Practices

Regular training on food safety, workplace safety, and employee rights helps staff understand compliance requirements. This reduces the risk of violations and promotes a safe and respectful work environment.

5. Establish a Relationship with Local Health Inspectors and Officials

Building a positive relationship with health inspectors, zoning officials, and labour regulators fosters open communication. Being proactive in addressing any concerns raised by these authorities can lead to smoother inspections and increased trust.

The Importance of Legal Compliance for Long-Term

Success

Legal and regulatory compliance is a foundational aspect of running a food business. By obtaining the necessary licenses, adhering to health and safety regulations, respecting employee rights, and complying with zoning ordinances, food entrepreneurs can build a reputable and sustainable business. Legal challenges, such as those faced by Chipotle and Shake Shack, demonstrate that non-compliance can lead to financial losses, reputational damage, and even legal action. However, with proactive planning, regular training, and collaboration with local authorities, these challenges can be managed effectively.

In the dynamic food industry, where regulations can vary widely and change frequently, staying informed and diligent is crucial. By making compliance a priority, food businesses can protect their customers, support their employees, and contribute positively to their communities.

CHAPTER 10: LOCATION STRATEGY FOR FOOD BUSINESSES

Choosing the right location is one of the most critical decisions a food entrepreneur can make. Whether for a brick-and-mortar restaurant, a food truck, or a pop-up event, location directly impacts visibility, customer accessibility, brand perception, and profitability. A well-chosen location not only attracts the target audience but can also serve as a valuable marketing tool, establishing a connection between the brand and its surroundings. This chapter explores the importance of location strategy for food businesses, outlines the factors to consider when assessing potential locations, and demonstrates how location can be leveraged as a powerful brand asset.

The Importance of Location for Food Businesses

The success of a food business is heavily influenced by its location. For brick-and-mortar restaurants, location affects visibility, customer access, and the likelihood of repeat business. For mobile food ventures, like food trucks, location strategy is more dynamic, as it involves selecting areas with high foot traffic or targeting events where the business's target audience is likely to be.

1. Brick-and-Mortar Restaurants

The location of a traditional restaurant can determine its visibility to passersby, ease of access, and appeal to a specific customer demographic. Restaurants in prime locations, such as bustling urban centres or popular tourist areas, often benefit from high foot traffic and increased brand visibility. However, these locations also come with higher rent and competition, making it essential to evaluate whether the increased cost aligns with the business's revenue potential.

- Example: Restaurants in shopping districts like New York's SoHo or San Francisco's Union Square gain exposure to large numbers of visitors, increasing the likelihood of foot traffic and brand visibility. While rent may be high, these locations offer significant marketing advantages by positioning the restaurant in a bustling, high-profile area.

2. Mobile Food Businesses (Food Trucks)

Mobile food businesses have the advantage of flexibility, allowing them to "follow the crowd" and adapt to seasonal or weekly variations in foot traffic. Location strategy for food trucks involves selecting high-traffic areas, such as business districts during lunch hours, events like music festivals, or popular parks on weekends. Choosing a regular route or schedule also helps establish consistency and customer familiarity.

- Example: In Los Angeles, food trucks often operate near corporate offices during lunch hours, then relocate to nightlife areas in the evening. This approach maximizes exposure to target customers at different times of day and increases profitability by capitalizing on peak demand.

3. Pop-Ups and Seasonal Locations

Pop-up restaurants and seasonal locations rely on temporary setups that often operate in unique or unconventional spaces, like art galleries, rooftop venues, or outdoor markets. The appeal of pop-ups lies in their exclusivity, and the chosen location can enhance the novelty factor, attracting food enthusiasts and creating a sense of urgency.

- Example: A pop-up bakery in San Francisco's Ferry Building Marketplace can draw high foot traffic from both locals and tourists. By offering a limited-time experience in a well-known venue, the bakery creates buzz and brand exposure without a long-term lease commitment.

Assessing Foot Traffic, Competition, and Local Demand

Selecting a location requires a thorough analysis of several factors, including foot traffic, competition, and local demand. Understanding these aspects allows entrepreneurs to identify sites that align with their target market, differentiate their brand from competitors, and maximize revenue potential.

1. Foot Traffic

Foot traffic refers to the number of people passing by a location, which is particularly important for food businesses that rely on walk-in customers. High foot traffic increases the likelihood of attracting new customers, but it's essential to assess whether the type of foot traffic aligns with the target demographic.

- Analysing Foot Traffic Patterns: Observing foot traffic at different times of day and week provides insights into peak hours and potential customer flow. For instance, business districts may experience high foot traffic during lunch hours, while nightlife areas peak in the evening.

- Data Sources: Tools like Placer.ai and Google Maps can provide foot traffic data, allowing entrepreneurs to evaluate potential locations quantitatively. In addition, conducting on-site observations and speaking with nearby business owners can provide practical insights.

- Example: A coffee shop located near a busy train station might experience high foot traffic during morning rush hours, catering to commuters who appreciate the convenience of grabbing coffee on their way to work.

2. Competition Analysis

Understanding the competitive landscape is crucial when selecting a location. While a certain level of competition can indicate demand, oversaturation may reduce a business's chances of success. Assessing nearby competitors allows entrepreneurs to identify gaps in the market and determine how their concept can stand out.

- Identifying Competitors: Entrepreneurs should research nearby food establishments to understand their menus, pricing, and target audiences. Analysing online reviews, social media presence, and customer feedback helps identify competitor strengths and weaknesses.

- Differentiating the Brand: A food business can differentiate itself by offering unique dishes, targeting underserved demographics, or enhancing customer experience. Identifying a gap in the market allows the business to position itself strategically in a competitive area.

- Example: In a neighbourhood with several high-end restaurants, a casual, affordable dining option could appeal to families and younger customers. By positioning itself as a laid-back alternative, the business can attract an audience looking for variety.

3. Local Demand and Demographics

Understanding the local demographic is essential for aligning the business with the preferences and needs of the community. Key factors to consider include age, income level, lifestyle preferences, and cultural diversity. Conducting a demographic analysis helps entrepreneurs tailor their concept to fit the area's unique profile.

- Assessing Customer Needs: Demographic data, such as census information, local surveys, and industry reports, provides insights into the preferences and spending habits of the community. For instance, a location with a large student population may prefer affordable, quick-service options, while affluent neighbourhoods may gravitate toward premium dining experiences.

- Cultural Relevance: Some neighbourhoods are known for specific culinary preferences or cultural significance, making it beneficial to align the menu with local tastes. For instance, a Mediterranean restaurant may thrive in an area with a strong Middle Eastern community, while a vegan café may find success in neighbourhoods known for health-conscious residents.

- Example: In Austin's South Congress district, known for its eclectic vibe and vibrant art scene, a fusion taco restaurant could attract both locals and tourists. By incorporating regional flavours and creating a unique dining experience, the restaurant aligns with the area's cultural appeal and eclectic customer base.

Using Location as a Marketing Asset

The location of a food business can become an integral part of its brand identity, helping attract customers and creating memorable dining experiences. By strategically choosing and designing the location, businesses can use it as a marketing asset to differentiate themselves from competitors and enhance customer loyalty.

1. Building a "Destination Location"

Some restaurants and cafés establish themselves as destination locations—places that customers go out of their way to visit because of the unique experience they offer. This approach often involves choosing an unusual or scenic location and creating an ambiance that amplifies the appeal.

- Unique Venues: Establishing a restaurant in an unusual venue, like a converted warehouse, historic building, or waterfront property, adds novelty to the dining experience. The ambiance created by the location can become a core part of the brand's identity, attracting customers who are looking for memorable experiences.

- Example: The Marina Social in Dubai is located along a waterfront promenade, offering stunning views of the city's marina. The combination of the scenic location and high-end dining makes it a "destination location" that attracts both locals and tourists.

2. Leveraging Location-Based Marketing

Location-based marketing uses digital tools to promote a business to customers nearby. By using GPS data, businesses can deliver targeted advertisements, promotions, or offers to people in the area, encouraging foot traffic and increasing visibility.

- Geotargeted Ads: Platforms like Google Ads and Facebook allow businesses to target ads to customers within a specific radius. These ads can promote daily specials, seasonal dishes, or exclusive discounts to attract nearby customers.

- Local Listings and SEO: Optimizing the business's online presence through local SEO and listings on platforms like Google My Business, Yelp, and TripAdvisor improves visibility in search results, making it easier for customers to find the business online.

- Example: A burger joint in a popular tourist district might use geotargeted ads to promote a limited-time "Tourist Special" to visitors in the area. This strategy not only attracts tourists but also reinforces the brand's relevance to the location.

3. Creating a Sense of Community Connection

Establishing a food business that connects with the

local community can strengthen brand loyalty and foster word-of-mouth marketing. By engaging with the neighbourhood, supporting local events, and sourcing ingredients locally, businesses create a sense of community that resonates with customers.

- Supporting Local Events and Causes: Sponsoring local festivals, hosting community gatherings, or collaborating with local artists and musicians makes the business more visible and embedded in the community.

- Emphasizing Local Ingredients: Highlighting locally sourced ingredients not only enhances the menu's appeal but also reinforces the connection between the restaurant and the area.

- Example: A farm-to-table restaurant in a suburban neighbourhood may emphasize its use of produce from nearby farms, attracting customers who value sustainability and local support. By participating in farmers' markets and community fairs, the restaurant establishes itself as a positive community presence.

Case Study: The Location Strategy of "Pike Place Chowder"

Pike Place Chowder, a renowned chowder restaurant in Seattle, exemplifies how location can play a vital role in a brand's success. Located in Pike Place Market, one of Seattle's most iconic tourist attractions, Pike Place Chowder benefits from the heavy foot traffic of both locals and visitors. By selecting a high-visibility location, the business leverages its proximity to the market to attract a constant flow of customers looking for an authentic Seattle dining experience.

1. Strategic Location Choice:

Pike Place Market attracts millions of visitors each year, making it a prime spot for a restaurant specializing in a regional dish like chowder. The location complements the brand by creating an association with Seattle's cultural identity and coastal heritage.

2. Creating a Destination Experience:

Pike Place Chowder has capitalized on its location to build a reputation as a must-visit destination for chowder lovers. The unique ambiance of Pike Place Market and the restaurant's high-quality, locally inspired menu make it a memorable experience, which has contributed to its popularity on social media and review platforms.

3. Leveraging Community Ties:

The restaurant sources ingredients from local vendors, reinforcing its commitment to the Seattle community and emphasizing the quality and freshness of its offerings. By integrating its brand with the local market, Pike Place Chowder has cultivated a loyal following that extends beyond tourists to Seattle residents who appreciate its community ties.

Crafting a Strategic Location Plan

For food entrepreneurs, location is much more than a physical address—it's a strategic asset that influences customer access, brand perception, and profitability. By carefully selecting a location, assessing factors like foot traffic, competition, and local demand, and leveraging location as a marketing tool, businesses can establish a strong foundation for success. Whether creating a destination location, using location-based marketing, or fostering community connections, a thoughtful location strategy contributes to long-term brand growth.

As seen with Pike Place Chowder, aligning location with brand identity and local culture enhances customer loyalty, fosters brand recognition, and drives repeat business. A strategic approach to location is essential for any food entrepreneur looking to create a lasting impact in their market.

CHAPTER 11: KITCHEN AND EQUIPMENT ESSENTIALS

The kitchen is the heart of any food business. An efficient, well-equipped kitchen not only supports the quality of food but also impacts productivity, safety, and cost management. Designing a kitchen that meets operational needs while remaining within budget is essential for every food entrepreneur. This chapter will explore the basics of kitchen design, essential equipment for various types of food businesses, the importance of balancing cost with quality and durability, and real-world examples of how efficient kitchen setups enhance productivity.

The Fundamentals of Kitchen Design

A well-planned kitchen design is crucial for ensuring smooth operations and minimizing bottlenecks. Kitchen layout, workflow, and space allocation directly impact employee efficiency, safety, and even food quality. To design an efficient kitchen, it's essential to understand different layout options, prioritize workflow, and consider specific needs based on the type of food business.

1. Choosing the Right Layout

Kitchen layout options vary based on the available space, the type of cuisine, and the volume of orders. Common kitchen layouts include:

- Assembly Line Layout: Ideal for quick-service restaurants and high-volume kitchens, this layout positions workstations in a straight line to streamline assembly. Each station is dedicated to a specific task (e.g., prepping, cooking, plating), allowing for a fast and efficient workflow.
- Island Layout: Often used in fine dining and high-end restaurants, this layout places the main cooking equipment (e.g., stoves, ovens) in a central island, surrounded by prep and plating stations. This design promotes communication and is conducive to open kitchen concepts.
- Zone Layout: This layout divides the kitchen into zones, each dedicated to a specific function (e.g., baking, frying, cold prep). Zone layouts work well in larger kitchens where different types of food require separate spaces to prevent cross-contamination.

- Example: Fast-casual chain Chipotle uses an assembly line layout in its open kitchens, where ingredients are prepped and assembled in a linear sequence. This layout enables employees to quickly build each order while ensuring consistency, speed, and minimal congestion.

2. Prioritizing Workflow and Safety

Efficient workflow is essential for reducing employee movement, minimizing wait times, and ensuring food is prepared consistently. When planning a kitchen layout, food entrepreneurs should consider the sequence of food preparation, from storage and prep to cooking and plating. Arranging workstations in a logical flow improves efficiency and reduces the risk of accidents.

- Work Triangle: In most kitchens, the work triangle (connecting the storage, preparation, and cooking areas) is fundamental for optimizing movement and reducing unnecessary steps. Placing these core areas within close proximity ensures quick access to ingredients and equipment.
- Safety Measures: Kitchen design must also incorporate safety measures, such as adequate space for movement, slip-resistant flooring, and clear pathways for hot food and waste disposal. Ensuring that fire extinguishers, first-aid kits, and emergency exits are accessible further enhances safety.
- Example: In a bakery, placing the prep area (for measuring and mixing) close to the ovens reduces travel time, while positioning storage for ingredients nearby ensures employees can easily access flour, sugar, and other staples. This layout maximizes efficiency while minimizing movement in a hot environment.

Essential Kitchen Equipment for Efficiency and Safety

Equipping the kitchen with essential, high-quality tools ensures consistent food quality and supports smooth operations. While equipment needs vary based on the type of food business, certain core items are necessary for most commercial kitchens.

1. Cooking Equipment

High-quality cooking equipment is the backbone of any food business, supporting a range of cooking methods and ensuring consistency.

- Range and Ovens: Ranges (stoves) and ovens are central to most kitchens. Convection ovens, which use fans to circulate heat, are particularly popular as they cook food evenly and quickly. For businesses focused on baking, specialized ovens like deck ovens or steam ovens may be necessary.
- Grills and Fryers: For fast-casual and quick-service restaurants, grills and fryers allow for quick preparation of popular items like burgers and fries. Countertop grills are often sufficient for food trucks and smaller kitchens, while larger establishments may require full-size grills and fryers.
- Induction Burners: Induction burners are energy-efficient and safer than traditional gas stoves, making them ideal for compact or mobile kitchens. They use magnetic fields to directly heat pots and pans, resulting in quick heating and minimal energy waste.

- Example: Burger chain Five Guys uses specialized flat-top grills in each location to ensure that burgers are cooked evenly and efficiently, maintaining consistency across all branches. The choice of durable, high-quality grills has become integral to their brand, as customers associate Five Guys with a distinct cooking style.

2. Refrigeration and Storage Solutions

Proper refrigeration and storage equipment are essential for food safety and efficiency. High-capacity refrigerators, freezers, and dry storage areas ensure ingredients are fresh and accessible.

- Walk-In Coolers and Freezers: Larger kitchens often require walk-in coolers and freezers, which provide ample storage space for perishable ingredients. Smaller establishments may use reach-in refrigerators that fit under counters to save space.
- Prep Tables with Refrigeration: Prep tables with built-in refrigeration compartments allow chefs to keep ingredients close at hand while preparing dishes. This setup is ideal for pizzerias, delis, and salad bars, where fresh ingredients are used continuously.
- Dry Storage: Dry storage areas are needed for non-perishable ingredients like grains, spices, and canned goods. Organized storage solutions, such as labelled bins and shelves, help keep the kitchen tidy and reduce food waste.

- Example: Subway utilizes prep tables with refrigerated compartments for fresh vegetables, sauces, and meats. This setup keeps ingredients organized and within reach, ensuring efficient sandwich assembly and minimizing wait times for customers.

3. Food Preparation Equipment

Efficient food preparation equipment, such as mixers, blenders, and slicers, supports consistency and reduces preparation time, especially in high-volume kitchens.

- Mixers and Food Processors: For bakeries, pizzerias, and restaurants that prepare dough or sauces in bulk, mixers and food processors save time and produce consistent results. Stand mixers with multiple attachments can handle various tasks, from kneading dough to whipping cream.

- Slicers and Dicers: Slicers and dicers help prepare ingredients quickly and consistently. They are particularly useful in fast-casual settings, where consistent portion sizes and uniform presentation are important.

- Blenders and Immersion Blenders: Blenders are essential for making soups, sauces, and smoothies. Immersion blenders, which can be used directly in pots, are convenient for pureeing soups and reducing cleanup time.

- Example: At Chipotle, commercial slicers are used to prepare ingredients like tomatoes and onions quickly and consistently, ensuring each batch is uniform. This equipment enables the staff to meet high customer demand without sacrificing quality.

4. Safety and Sanitation Equipment

Maintaining cleanliness and safety is essential in any food business. Proper sanitation equipment and tools reduce the risk of foodborne illnesses and maintain a safe environment for employees.

- Hand-Washing Stations: Designated hand-washing stations with soap, hand sanitizers, and disposable towels are mandatory for hygiene compliance. Conveniently placed stations encourage regular hand-washing among staff.

- Dishwashers and Sanitizing Stations: Commercial dishwashers sanitize dishes quickly and effectively, making them indispensable for high-volume kitchens. Sanitizing stations for cleaning tools and utensils further enhance hygiene.

- Safety Equipment: Items like fire extinguishers, first-aid kits, and non-slip mats promote safety. Proper ventilation systems are also crucial in preventing heat buildup, reducing smoke, and eliminating odours.

- Example: In high-volume kitchens like McDonald's, dishwashing stations are designed for quick turnover, allowing for efficient cleaning and sterilization of dishes and utensils, reducing wait times, and ensuring consistent sanitation.

Balancing Cost, Quality, and Durability in Equipment Selection

Investing in quality equipment is essential for long-term efficiency and cost-effectiveness. While it may be tempting to cut costs by purchasing cheaper equipment, doing so often leads to higher maintenance expenses and frequent replacements. Striking a balance between cost, quality, and durability helps ensure the kitchen operates smoothly and remains profitable.

1. Prioritizing High-Use Equipment

High-use equipment, such as stoves, ovens, and refrigerators, should be of high quality and durability, as these items are used daily and must withstand heavy wear and tear. Investing in premium equipment for high-use items reduces the likelihood of breakdowns and extends the equipment's lifespan.

- Example: For a coffee shop, purchasing a high-quality espresso machine is a worthwhile investment. This machine will be used frequently, and a durable, efficient model can enhance beverage quality and reduce the need for costly repairs.

2. Leasing vs. Purchasing Equipment

Leasing equipment is an option that allows food businesses to conserve upfront capital and try equipment before committing to ownership. While leasing involves monthly payments, it may be more affordable for startups that need to manage cash flow.

- Advantages of Leasing: Lower initial costs, access to newer models, and flexibility to upgrade as needed.
- Advantages of Purchasing: Long-term savings, asset ownership, and no ongoing rental fees.
- Example: A new food truck may lease its commercial-grade refrigerator, allowing it to test the equipment's efficiency before deciding to purchase. Leasing also reduces initial expenses, which is beneficial for new businesses working with limited budgets.

3. Considering Energy Efficiency

Energy-efficient equipment helps reduce utility costs, making it a cost-effective choice in the long run. Energy Star-rated appliances, for instance, consume less electricity and can result in significant savings over time.

- Example: A bakery that invests in an energy-efficient convection oven can save on electricity while benefiting from the oven's fast, even heating capabilities. These savings can add up, especially in businesses where ovens are used continuously.

Examples of How Efficient Kitchen Setups Improve Productivity

An efficiently designed kitchen setup has a direct impact on productivity, allowing staff to move seamlessly between tasks, reduce preparation time, and improve service speed.

1. Example: Fast-Food Chain Efficiency – McDonald's "Speedee Service System"

McDonald's introduced the "Speedee Service System" in the 1940s, a kitchen layout designed to maximize efficiency by breaking down the food preparation process into simple, repeatable steps. By dividing tasks into specific stations—such as grilling, assembling, and wrapping—McDonald's achieved unparalleled speed and consistency. This streamlined system has become a model for fast-food kitchens worldwide, demonstrating how efficient layouts can increase productivity and customer satisfaction.

2. Example: Open Kitchen Efficiency – Chipotle's Assembly Line

Chipotle's open kitchen and assembly line model allow customers to see each step of their meal preparation while ensuring efficiency. Employees at each station are responsible for specific tasks, such as preparing burrito fillings, adding toppings, and wrapping orders. This setup reduces order time and ensures consistent quality, helping Chipotle serve high volumes of customers quickly.

3. Example: High-Volume Catering – Efficient Storage and Prep Stations

For catering companies, where large volumes of food are prepared in advance, an efficient kitchen setup involves ample prep stations, storage, and a well-organized assembly line. By grouping prep tables, refrigeration units, and packaging areas, catering businesses can streamline their workflow and manage large orders without compromising quality.

- Example: A catering company specializing in events maintains multiple prep stations with pre-portioned ingredients. This setup minimizes preparation time on-site, allowing staff to focus on plating and serving at the event, ensuring a smooth and timely presentation.

Creating an Effective Kitchen Strategy

A well-equipped and efficiently designed kitchen is essential for the success of any food business. By prioritizing workflow, investing in quality equipment, and selecting layouts that support operational needs, food entrepreneurs can create a kitchen that promotes productivity, safety, and consistent food quality. Whether in a high-volume fast-food setting, a boutique coffee shop, or a mobile food truck, an efficient kitchen setup helps the business achieve its goals and enhances the overall customer experience.

The examples from McDonald's, Chipotle, and catering setups illustrate how efficient kitchen designs improve productivity and customer satisfaction, providing a blueprint for food entrepreneurs to optimize their kitchen spaces. With thoughtful planning and strategic investment in essential equipment, food businesses can build a kitchen that meets the demands of their unique operations and supports long-term success.

CHAPTER 12: SOURCING INGREDIENTS AND SUPPLIER MANAGEMENT

The ingredients used in a food business directly impact the quality of dishes, customer satisfaction, and overall brand reputation. As consumer demand for fresh, high-quality, and ethically sourced ingredients increases, food entrepreneurs face the challenge of balancing quality with cost and supply consistency. This chapter explores the importance of sourcing high-quality ingredients, strategies for building and managing supplier relationships, and considerations for choosing between local and international suppliers. We'll also delve into the growing trend of sustainable procurement and its advantages in creating a responsible, resilient food business.

The Importance of Quality Ingredients in Customer Satisfaction

High-quality ingredients are the foundation of any successful food business, as they enhance flavour, nutritional value, and presentation. Customers today are more discerning than ever, often seeking out establishments that prioritize fresh, locally sourced, or organic ingredients. In many cases, quality ingredients can elevate a dish from ordinary to exceptional, distinguishing a brand from its competitors.

1. Flavour and Freshness

Fresh ingredients contribute to superior flavour and texture, making dishes more appealing and enjoyable. Quality ingredients tend to require fewer additives and preservatives, allowing natural flavours to shine. By prioritizing freshness, food businesses can ensure that every meal meets or exceeds customer expectations, fostering positive reviews and word-of-mouth recommendations.

- Example: Many Italian restaurants emphasize the use of fresh, high-quality tomatoes, basil, and olive oil to create authentic pasta sauces with rich flavours. By sourcing fresh ingredients, these establishments can deliver a dining experience that resonates with customers' taste expectations.

2. Nutritional Value and Health Appeal

The nutritional content of ingredients is an increasingly important factor for health-conscious customers. Organic produce, grass-fed meats, and minimally processed ingredients offer health benefits that appeal to consumers looking to make healthier food choices. Establishments that emphasize wholesome, nutrient-dense ingredients often attract loyal customers who prioritize quality in their diets.

- Example: Sweetgreen, a popular salad chain, markets itself on using fresh, organic produce and antibiotic-free meats. This emphasis on nutrition and quality has helped Sweetgreen build a strong customer base among health-conscious diners.

3. Brand Reputation and Customer Loyalty

Quality ingredients contribute to brand reputation, as customers associate the freshness and flavour of food with the brand itself. Businesses that consistently deliver high-quality dishes can build trust and loyalty, while those that compromise on ingredient quality risk disappointing customers and damaging their reputation.

- Example: Farm-to-table restaurant Blue Hill in New York has cultivated a reputation for using sustainably sourced, high-quality ingredients. Its commitment to freshness and transparency attracts diners who appreciate culinary excellence and ethical sourcing, resulting in a dedicated clientele.

Building and Managing Supplier Relationships for Consistency

Establishing strong, reliable relationships with suppliers is crucial for maintaining ingredient quality and consistency. A dependable supply chain allows food businesses to ensure that ingredients meet their quality standards, are delivered on time, and are available consistently.

1. Selecting the Right Suppliers

Choosing the right suppliers involves assessing several factors, including product quality, pricing, delivery schedules, and the supplier's reputation. Conducting research, reviewing testimonials, and asking for references can help food entrepreneurs identify suppliers that align with their brand's standards and values.

- Quality Assurance: Work with suppliers that implement strict quality control measures to ensure consistency. Certifications, such as organic or fair trade, can offer an additional layer of assurance for businesses focusing on specific product standards.

- Reliability: Reliable suppliers prioritize timely deliveries and transparent communication, which helps prevent disruptions in the supply chain. Many food businesses enter into agreements with multiple suppliers to ensure they have backup options if their primary supplier experiences issues.

- Example: High-end seafood restaurants often partner with trusted fishmongers to source fresh, high-quality seafood daily. These suppliers may offer customized services, such as preparing and portioning the fish, to streamline operations and meet the restaurant's specific needs.

2. Maintaining Open Communication

Strong supplier relationships rely on clear, consistent communication. Regular check-ins, clear product specifications, and feedback on performance help build a collaborative partnership. By keeping communication channels open, businesses can address potential issues proactively, ensuring a stable supply chain.

- Setting Clear Expectations: Provide suppliers with detailed information about quality standards, preferred packaging, delivery schedules, and any specific requirements. A written agreement helps clarify these expectations and holds both parties accountable.
- Feedback and Transparency: Openly discussing concerns or improvements fosters trust and mutual respect. Providing feedback on product quality, delivery timeliness, or customer response can help suppliers fine-tune their services to better meet the business's needs.
- Example: A coffee shop chain might regularly communicate with its coffee bean suppliers to discuss seasonal changes in flavour profiles or adjust roast levels based on customer feedback. This collaborative approach allows both parties to maintain high standards and adapt to evolving consumer tastes.

3. Negotiating Terms and Building Long-Term Partnerships

Building a long-term relationship with suppliers often results in mutually beneficial terms, such as competitive pricing, flexible delivery options, or preferential treatment during supply shortages. Negotiating favourable terms and establishing strong rapport with suppliers can lead to cost savings and greater security in the supply chain.

- Loyalty Incentives: Many suppliers offer loyalty

incentives, such as discounts or exclusive access to limited products, to long-term clients. Food businesses can leverage these benefits to improve profitability or offer seasonal, specialty items to customers.

- Shared Values and Goals: Aligning with suppliers who share similar values—such as sustainability, ethical sourcing, or local support—reinforces brand integrity and promotes a collaborative, long-lasting partnership.

- Example: Whole Foods Market cultivates strong relationships with local farmers, providing them with consistent business and support. In return, the farmers supply fresh produce that meets Whole Foods' quality and sustainability standards, creating a mutually beneficial partnership.

Local vs. International Sourcing and Sustainable Procurement Options

Food entrepreneurs must decide between sourcing ingredients locally or internationally, each with distinct advantages and challenges. In recent years, sustainable sourcing has become a priority, as businesses seek to minimize environmental impact, support ethical practices, and appeal to eco-conscious consumers.

1. Local Sourcing

Sourcing ingredients locally offers several benefits, including fresher products, reduced transportation costs, and a lower environmental footprint. Local sourcing also supports the community by fostering relationships with nearby farmers and producers.

- Advantages: Local ingredients are fresher, seasonal,

and often have a smaller carbon footprint. Supporting local suppliers strengthens community ties and can be an attractive selling point for customers who value regional flavours and sustainability.

- Challenges: Local sourcing can be limited by seasonality, especially in areas with harsh winters or dry climates. Additionally, local products may sometimes be more expensive due to smaller-scale production.

- Example: Chef Alice Waters' restaurant Chez Panisse has become renowned for its commitment to local, seasonal ingredients sourced from California farmers. This dedication to local sourcing has positioned Chez Panisse as a pioneer in the farm-to-table movement, inspiring a nationwide trend.

2. International Sourcing

International sourcing allows food businesses to access unique ingredients and maintain menu consistency year-round. Specialty products, such as exotic spices, tropical fruits, and imported cheeses, are often sourced internationally to achieve authentic flavours.

- Advantages: International sourcing provides access to a broader variety of ingredients, enabling restaurants to create globally inspired dishes. For businesses with international concepts, sourcing specific ingredients from their countries of origin can enhance authenticity.

- Challenges: International sourcing involves longer shipping times, increased environmental impact, and potential import fees or tariffs. Additionally, global supply chains are vulnerable to disruptions, such as political changes or weather-related delays.

- Example: A sushi restaurant may import premium-grade fish from Japan to ensure the highest quality for its dishes. By sourcing fish directly from Japanese suppliers, the restaurant enhances its authenticity and meets customer expectations for traditional flavours.

3. Sustainable Procurement

Sustainable sourcing focuses on reducing environmental impact and supporting ethical practices, such as fair labour and animal welfare. Consumers increasingly favour brands that demonstrate social and environmental responsibility, making sustainable procurement a valuable differentiator in the market.

- Eco-Friendly Certifications: Certifications like Fair Trade, Rainforest Alliance, and USDA Organic indicate that products meet specific sustainability standards. Many customers seek out these labels, as they assure transparency and responsible sourcing practices.
- Ethical Partnerships: Partnering with suppliers that prioritize fair wages, humane treatment of animals, and environmental conservation reinforces a brand's ethical values and resonates with eco-conscious consumers.
- Example: Chipotle sources sustainably raised meats and organic produce, positioning itself as a responsible brand that prioritizes quality and ethical sourcing. This commitment to sustainability not only enhances Chipotle's brand image but also appeals to customers who value transparency and social responsibility.

Case Study: Sustainable Sourcing at Sweetgreen

Sweetgreen, a fast-casual salad chain, exemplifies the benefits of sustainable sourcing and supplier relationship management. The brand prioritizes locally sourced, organic ingredients, working closely with farmers to ensure freshness and sustainability. Here's how Sweetgreen's approach to sourcing has contributed to its success:

1. Commitment to Local and Seasonal Ingredients:

Sweetgreen sources much of its produce from local farms, emphasizing seasonal ingredients that reflect regional flavours. This approach not only supports local agriculture but also reduces the environmental impact of long-distance transportation.

2. Transparent Supplier Partnerships:

Sweetgreen maintains close relationships with its suppliers, providing transparency about where its ingredients come from and how they're grown. By highlighting these partnerships on its menu and website, Sweetgreen builds trust with customers who appreciate knowing the origins of their food.

3. Customer Loyalty Through Sustainability:

Sweetgreen's dedication to sustainable sourcing has earned it a loyal customer base among health-conscious, eco-friendly consumers. The company's commitment to quality ingredients and ethical practices resonates with customers who value responsible dining choices.

Practical Tips for Effective Ingredient Sourcing and Supplier Management

1. Diversify Your Supplier Network

Working with multiple suppliers for critical ingredients reduces dependency on a single source, making the business more resilient to supply chain disruptions. A diversified supplier network provides backup options if primary suppliers experience shortages or delays.

2. Conduct Regular Quality Audits

Regular audits of supplier quality ensure that ingredients consistently meet the business's standards. Conduct on-site visits if possible, review product samples, and monitor supplier performance over time to maintain high standards.

3. Use Technology for Inventory and Ordering

Inventory management software helps track ingredient levels, monitor expiration dates, and optimize order quantities. By automating ordering processes, food businesses can maintain sufficient stock without over-ordering, reducing waste and costs.

4. Stay Informed About Market Trends

Monitoring market trends, such as price fluctuations or new product offerings, allows businesses to anticipate changes in ingredient costs and availability. Staying informed enables proactive adjustments to menus or sourcing strategies, reducing the impact of sudden price spikes.

Building a Resilient Sourcing Strategy

Sourcing high-quality ingredients and managing

supplier relationships are integral to the success of any food business. By prioritizing ingredient quality, establishing strong supplier partnerships, and considering sustainable procurement options, food entrepreneurs can build a reliable, ethical, and resilient supply chain. Whether choosing local farms or international providers, a strategic approach to sourcing enhances customer satisfaction, supports brand reputation, and promotes long-term sustainability.

As illustrated by Sweetgreen's approach, a commitment to quality and transparency can lead to loyal customers who value responsible sourcing. By implementing effective supplier management practices and exploring sustainable options, food businesses can create a supply chain that supports their values, meets customer expectations, and strengthens their brand in a competitive market.

CHAPTER 13: MENU DEVELOPMENT AND PRICING STRATEGY

Developing an appealing and profitable menu is a fundamental part of establishing a successful food business. A thoughtfully designed menu reflects the brand's identity, meets the preferences of the target audience, and strategically balances creativity with profitability. Pricing strategy plays a critical role in this process, influencing customer perception, sales volume, and overall profit margins. In this chapter, we will explore how to create a menu that aligns with the brand, examine various pricing techniques, and gain insights from culinary consultants on crafting a profitable menu that resonates with customers.

Creating a Menu that Aligns with the Brand and Appeals to the Target Market

The menu is one of the most powerful tools for defining

a food business's brand. It not only sets the tone for the dining experience but also serves as a direct communication channel to the customer, conveying the business's culinary values, level of innovation, and target demographic.

1. Understanding the Brand Identity

A menu should reflect the core elements of the brand, such as cuisine style, service approach, and values. For example, a health-focused café would emphasize fresh, organic ingredients and plant-based options, while a high-end steakhouse would focus on premium cuts and sophisticated presentations.

- Consistent Theme and Language: The tone, language, and descriptions used on the menu should be consistent with the brand. A casual burger joint might use fun, playful language, while a fine dining restaurant would opt for elegant descriptions that highlight ingredient origins and preparation techniques.

- Visual Elements: Menu design, including font, colours, and layout, should visually align with the brand. For instance, a rustic, farm-to-table restaurant might use earthy tones and handwritten-style fonts to convey authenticity and simplicity.

- Example: Shake Shack's menu is designed to reflect a casual, fast-casual dining experience with simple, playful language and minimalist design. The focus on high-quality ingredients in an accessible format aligns with the brand's image, appealing to a broad demographic of fast-casual diners.

2. Catering to the Target Audience

Understanding the preferences and needs of the target market is essential for creating a menu that resonates with customers. Demographic factors, such as age, income level, and dietary habits, influence menu choices and pricing strategies.

- Health-Conscious and Dietary Needs: For health-conscious customers, offering options like low-calorie, gluten-free, and vegan dishes is important. Clear labelling and detailed ingredient information cater to diners with specific dietary preferences.
- Regional and Cultural Relevance: In areas with strong cultural communities, incorporating local or traditional flavours can increase the menu's appeal. Alternatively, in cosmopolitan areas, fusion dishes or globally inspired flavours can attract a diverse customer base.
- Example: At Sweetgreen, the menu includes a variety of healthy, customizable salad and bowl options, designed to appeal to health-conscious consumers, especially millennials. Seasonal ingredients and rotating menu items add excitement and encourage repeat visits.

3. Creating Signature Dishes

Signature dishes set a food business apart from competitors and give customers a reason to return. These dishes reflect the brand's unique approach and culinary creativity, becoming closely associated with the business's identity.

- Highlighting Special Ingredients: Using high-quality or unique ingredients in signature dishes reinforces the brand's dedication to quality and innovation.
- Storytelling: Incorporating a backstory or cultural

significance behind a signature dish can make it more memorable, adding emotional value for the customer.

- Example: The "Original ShackBurger" at Shake Shack is a signature item that has become synonymous with the brand. Its focus on quality beef, simplicity, and distinctive flavour profile sets it apart in the competitive burger market.

Pricing Techniques: Cost-Based, Competition-Based, and Value-Based Pricing

Pricing is a complex but critical element of menu development, as it directly impacts profitability and customer perceptions. Selecting the right pricing strategy depends on various factors, including target market expectations, ingredient costs, and brand positioning.

1. Cost-Based Pricing

Cost-based pricing, also known as cost-plus pricing, involves setting menu prices based on the cost of ingredients, labour, and overhead, with a markup added to achieve the desired profit margin. This straightforward approach ensures that all costs are covered while generating a profit.

- Determining Ingredient Costs: Calculate the total cost of each dish by factoring in ingredient prices, portion sizes, and preparation time. Some businesses use food cost calculators to simplify this process.
- Setting a Markup: Add a markup that covers operating costs and desired profit margin. For example, if the total cost per dish is $5, a 300% markup would result in a $15

menu price.

- Advantages: Cost-based pricing provides clear insight into profitability and is straightforward to calculate.

- Challenges: This approach may not fully account for customer perceptions or competitive pricing, potentially resulting in prices that are either too high or too low.

- Example: Many quick-service restaurants use cost-based pricing to ensure profitability while keeping prices affordable. By keeping food costs to around 30% of the selling price, they balance quality with affordability.

2. Competition-Based Pricing

Competition-based pricing involves setting prices based on what competitors are charging for similar items. This approach is common in areas with high competition, where customers have multiple dining options and tend to compare prices.

- Benchmarking Against Competitors: Analyse the menus of nearby competitors to understand average pricing for similar items. This helps establish price points that are competitive within the local market.

- Differentiating with Value Additions: Businesses using competition-based pricing often look for ways to differentiate their offerings, such as larger portions, unique flavours, or higher-quality ingredients, to justify slightly higher prices.

- Advantages: This method helps businesses remain competitive and meet customer expectations for price.

- Challenges: Competitive pricing may limit profit margins and doesn't account for unique aspects of the business's offerings or target market preferences.

- Example: Many coffee shops price their espresso drinks similarly to competitors in the area but may differentiate themselves through unique flavours or better-quality beans.

3. Value-Based Pricing

Value-based pricing is centred around the perceived value of the product or experience from the customer's perspective. This approach allows businesses to set higher prices for unique or premium offerings, as customers are willing to pay more for perceived value.

- Highlighting Unique Value Propositions: Emphasizing special ingredients, culinary expertise, ambiance, or exceptional service can justify higher prices. Value-based pricing works well for businesses that provide a unique experience or specialized cuisine.

- Customer-Centric Pricing: By understanding customer demographics and preferences, food businesses can set prices that reflect what their target audience is willing to pay for quality, exclusivity, or convenience.

- Advantages: Value-based pricing allows for higher profit margins and emphasizes the business's unique strengths.

- Challenges: This approach requires a strong understanding of the customer base and may not work in highly competitive, price-sensitive markets.

- Example: Fine dining restaurants often use value-based pricing to reflect the exclusivity, ambiance, and expertise they provide. A high-end steakhouse, for instance, may charge premium prices for prime cuts and personalized service.

Insights from Culinary Consultants on Creating a Profitable Menu

Experienced culinary consultants offer valuable insights on balancing creativity with profitability, maintaining consistency, and using menu engineering to maximize revenue. Below are some best practices recommended by industry experts for designing a profitable menu.

1. Menu Engineering and Strategic Layout

Menu engineering involves analysing menu items based on popularity and profitability, then strategically placing them on the menu to maximize revenue. This approach helps identify high-margin items and encourages customers to order them.

- Highlighting High-Profit Items: Place high-margin dishes in prominent menu positions, such as the top right corner, where customers are more likely to look first.

- Using Descriptive Language: Vivid descriptions and appetizing adjectives can make dishes more appealing, increasing the likelihood of customer selection.

- Example: A restaurant might highlight a profitable "Chef's Special" with a detailed description of its unique ingredients and preparation. This draws attention to the dish and encourages customers to try it, enhancing profitability.

2. Balancing Creativity with Consistency

While creative dishes and seasonal items attract customer interest, consistency is key to building a loyal customer base. Culinary consultants often advise that core menu items should remain consistent in quality and availability, even as seasonal specials are introduced.

- Core vs. Seasonal Items: Keep a core set of popular dishes available year-round, while rotating seasonal or experimental items. This approach caters to both regular customers and those seeking novelty.
- Portion Control: Consistent portion sizes ensure that costs are controlled and that customers receive the same experience each time they visit, reinforcing brand reliability.

- Example: Panera Bread offers seasonal soups and salads but keeps its core menu items like the "Broccoli Cheddar Soup" available year-round. This balance appeals to both regular customers and those interested in seasonal flavours.

3. Optimizing Ingredient Usage for Cost Control

Culinary consultants emphasize the importance of optimizing ingredient usage to control costs and reduce waste. Efficient ingredient sourcing and repurposing unused ingredients across multiple dishes can improve profitability.

- Cross-Utilization of Ingredients: Using the same ingredients across multiple dishes reduces inventory costs. For example, tomatoes might be used in salads, sauces, and soups.
- Seasonal Ingredients for Lower Costs: Seasonal ingredients are often more affordable and fresher than out-of-season imports. Designing menu items around seasonal ingredients can reduce costs while enhancing flavour.

- Example: A Mediterranean restaurant might use chickpeas in salads, hummus, and stews, maximizing ingredient use and reducing waste.

This efficiency lowers costs while maintaining variety on the menu.

4. Regular Menu Analysis and Updates

Analysing menu performance regularly helps identify which dishes are profitable, which ones are underperforming, and where adjustments may be necessary. By tracking sales data and customer feedback, businesses can optimize their menu based on actual demand.

- Removing Low-Performing Items: Dishes that are expensive to prepare but unpopular with customers can be removed to streamline operations and improve profitability.
- Testing New Items: Introducing new items as limited-time offers allows businesses to gauge customer interest without committing to permanent menu changes. This approach encourages experimentation while reducing risk.

- Example: Fast-food chain McDonald's often introduces limited-time items, like the "McRib," to assess demand and increase excitement. Customer response determines whether items are added to the regular menu or remain seasonal offerings.

Crafting a Menu that Maximizes Appeal and Profitability

Developing a successful menu requires a strategic

balance of brand alignment, customer appeal, and profitability. By understanding the target market, creating signature dishes, and selecting an effective pricing strategy, food entrepreneurs can design a menu that resonates with customers and supports business growth. Culinary consultants' insights on menu engineering, ingredient optimization, and regular analysis further enhance profitability by maximizing efficiency and customer satisfaction.

As demonstrated by brands like Sweetgreen, Shake Shack, and Panera Bread, thoughtful menu development and pricing strategies foster brand loyalty, attract diverse customer demographics, and drive revenue. A well-crafted menu acts as both a brand ambassador and a revenue engine, helping food businesses thrive in a competitive landscape.

CHAPTER 14: MANAGING INVENTORY AND MINIMIZING WASTE

Efficient inventory management and waste reduction are essential for a food business's profitability and sustainability. By carefully tracking inventory, minimizing waste, and controlling costs, food entrepreneurs can maximize revenue, improve operational efficiency, and enhance their environmental responsibility. In this chapter, we will explore the basics of inventory management, introduce techniques to minimize food waste, and provide real-world examples of sustainable inventory practices that have proven effective in the industry.

The Basics of Inventory Management and Tracking Systems

Inventory management is the process of tracking and controlling stock, including ingredients, supplies, and packaging. In the food industry, effective inventory management ensures that ingredients are fresh, food costs remain within budget, and waste is minimized. It also enables businesses to avoid overstocking or running out of essential ingredients, both of which can impact profitability and customer satisfaction.

1. Establishing an Inventory Management System

An inventory management system helps track stock levels, monitor usage, and control reorder points. Systems can range from manual tracking methods, like spreadsheets, to more advanced software solutions that offer real-time tracking and analytics.

- Manual Tracking: Small establishments may use manual systems, such as spreadsheets or written logs, to track inventory. This method requires consistent recording but can be time-consuming and prone to errors.

- Inventory Management Software: For larger or high-volume operations, digital inventory management software offers real-time tracking, automatic reorder notifications, and data analytics. Software like Upserve, MarketMan, and BevSpot streamlines inventory tracking, improves accuracy, and enables better forecasting.

- Example: MarketMan is an inventory management software that allows restaurants to monitor stock levels, track ingredient usage, and generate reports on food costs. By automating inventory tracking, businesses can avoid stockouts and reduce overordering, improving cost control.

2. Tracking Inventory Turnover

Inventory turnover rate refers to how quickly stock is used and replaced. Monitoring turnover helps identify fast-moving versus slow-moving items, allowing businesses to adjust ordering patterns and avoid overstocking perishable goods.

- High Turnover Items: Items with high turnover, such as staple ingredients or popular menu items, should be monitored closely to ensure consistent availability.

- Slow-Moving Items: Ingredients that have a low turnover rate may be overstocked, leading to waste if they spoil. Adjusting order quantities or incorporating these ingredients into specials can help manage stock more effectively.

- Example: A bakery may find that flour and sugar have high turnover, while specialty ingredients like saffron are used less frequently. By tracking turnover, the bakery can order larger quantities of staples while limiting the amount of specialty ingredients to avoid waste.

3. Setting Par Levels and Reorder Points

Par levels represent the ideal amount of stock needed to meet demand without overstocking, while reorder points indicate when it's time to place a new order. Establishing par levels and reorder points helps streamline purchasing and prevents running out of essential items.

- Calculating Par Levels: Par levels are based on average usage rates, lead time for delivery, and safety stock. Adjusting these levels based on historical data ensures that stock is available without excessive surplus.

- Setting Reorder Points: Reorder points trigger new orders before stock runs out, accounting for delivery lead times. Automated systems can send alerts when items reach their reorder point, reducing the risk of shortages.

- Example: A coffee shop may set a par level of 50 pounds of coffee beans, with a reorder point of 20 pounds, ensuring that they have enough beans to meet demand while allowing time for new deliveries.

Techniques to Minimize Food Waste and Control Costs

Food waste can significantly impact a food business's profitability and environmental footprint. Reducing waste not only lowers costs but also aligns with sustainability values that resonate with customers. Here are some practical techniques for minimizing food waste and controlling costs.

1. Accurate Portion Control

Consistent portion sizes help manage inventory, control costs, and reduce waste by ensuring that ingredients are used efficiently. By standardizing portions, businesses can maintain consistency in their dishes and prevent overuse of ingredients.

- Weighing Ingredients: Using scales to measure ingredients ensures that portions are accurate, especially for high-cost items like meat or seafood.
- Training Staff on Portion Sizes: Educating staff on portion sizes helps prevent over-serving, particularly in high-turnover items where even small inconsistencies can lead to significant waste over time.

- Example: Chipotle trains employees on precise portioning for each ingredient in burritos and bowls. This practice ensures consistency in each order, controls costs, and minimizes waste while delivering a predictable product.

2. Implementing a "First-In, First-Out" (FIFO) System

The FIFO system ensures that older stock is used before newer items, reducing the likelihood of spoilage and waste. Proper labelling and organization are essential for implementing FIFO effectively.

- Labelling and Date Management: Label items with their purchase date and organize shelves so that older stock is at the front and used first.
- Rotating Stock Regularly: Regularly checking and rotating stock ensures that ingredients don't expire unnoticed. Designating specific staff members to oversee inventory rotation can improve accountability.
- Example: A restaurant that stores produce in FIFO order reduces waste by ensuring that older ingredients are used first. For instance, tomatoes delivered on Monday are used before those delivered on Wednesday.

3. Repurposing Ingredients and Creative Menu Planning

Repurposing ingredients can reduce waste by incorporating leftover or surplus items into new dishes or daily specials. This technique requires creativity and flexibility but can enhance the menu's variety and minimize waste.

- Daily Specials with Surplus Ingredients: When certain ingredients are nearing their expiration, incorporating them into a daily special prevents waste while offering customers something unique.

- Cross-Utilization of Ingredients: Using ingredients across multiple dishes reduces waste and optimizes usage. For instance, herbs used in sauces can also garnish plates, while bread nearing expiration can be made into croutons.

- Example: Panera Bread uses day-old bread to create croutons and breadcrumbs for soups and salads. This approach reduces waste while adding value to menu items.

4. Monitoring and Analysing Waste Patterns

Tracking waste helps identify patterns and areas for improvement. Waste logs can provide insight into why certain ingredients go unused, whether due to overordering, prep errors, or changing customer preferences.

- Waste Log Sheets: Documenting daily waste, including spoiled ingredients, uneaten meals, and prep errors, reveals recurring issues and helps identify solutions.
- Adjusting Orders Based on Data: Analysing waste data over time allows businesses to refine their ordering processes, reducing waste and controlling costs. Seasonal fluctuations in demand should also be considered.

- Example: A fast-casual restaurant might discover that lettuce waste spikes in winter when fewer salads are ordered. Reducing lettuce orders during colder months minimizes waste and cuts costs.

5. Leveraging Technology for Inventory Optimization

Digital inventory tools can help businesses track stock levels, predict demand, and adjust orders automatically. Advanced software solutions provide real-time data on inventory, allowing for smarter ordering and improved waste management.

- Forecasting Demand with Sales Data: Inventory software can analyse past sales data to predict demand and adjust orders accordingly. Seasonal adjustments help align inventory with customer preferences.
- Automatic Alerts for Expiring Stock: Some systems offer alerts for ingredients approaching expiration, enabling businesses to use them promptly and prevent spoilage.
- Example: A high-end restaurant uses forecasting software to manage perishable ingredients like seafood. By analysing sales trends, the software adjusts orders based on expected demand, reducing the risk of waste.

Real-World Examples of Sustainable Inventory Practices

Several food businesses have implemented sustainable inventory practices to reduce waste, control costs, and support their brand values. Here are some examples that demonstrate effective approaches to inventory management and waste reduction.

1. Blue Hill's "Waste Not" Approach

Blue Hill, a farm-to-table restaurant in New York, is known for its innovative approach to reducing waste. The restaurant's "Waste Not" menu repurposes food byproducts that would typically go unused, such as vegetable peels, stale bread, and offcuts of meat. By turning waste into creative dishes, Blue Hill reduces its environmental impact and educates diners about sustainable food practices.

- Sustainable Sourcing: Blue Hill works closely with local farms to source ingredients, emphasizing sustainable and regenerative farming practices. This approach minimizes waste by supporting a closed-loop food system.
- Educating Diners: Blue Hill's focus on repurposing food waste resonates with eco-conscious diners, who appreciate the restaurant's commitment to sustainability and creative use of ingredients.

2. Imperfect Produce at Misfits Market

Misfits Market, a subscription-based food delivery service, sources "imperfect" produce that would typically be discarded due to cosmetic imperfections. By partnering with farmers to buy surplus or irregular produce, Misfits Market reduces food waste and provides customers with affordable, sustainable food options.

- Reducing Food Waste at the Source: Misfits Market diverts perfectly edible but visually imperfect produce from going to waste. This sustainable model reduces environmental impact while supporting farmers.
- Cost Savings for Customers: By selling imperfect produce at discounted rates, Misfits Market appeals to cost-conscious consumers while promoting sustainable eating habits.

3. Starbucks' FoodShare Program

Starbucks has implemented the FoodShare program,

which donates unsold food to local food banks at the end of each day. This initiative prevents waste by repurposing surplus food, ensuring that items don't end up in landfills while helping feed those in need.

- Logistics for Food Donations: Starbucks works with nonprofit organizations to handle logistics and distribution. The program operates in multiple cities, helping the company minimize waste while giving back to the community.

- Positive Brand Impact: FoodShare aligns with Starbucks' social responsibility goals, improving public perception and highlighting the company's commitment to reducing waste.

4. Leanpath Technology in Corporate Kitchens

Leanpath is a food waste tracking technology used by corporate kitchens and large-scale dining facilities. The system monitors food waste in real-time, providing data on the types and quantities of ingredients wasted. By analysing this data, businesses can adjust purchasing and preparation processes to reduce waste.

- Data-Driven Waste Reduction: Leanpath's detailed waste tracking allows kitchen staff to identify inefficiencies and make targeted improvements, reducing costs and waste simultaneously.

- Employee Engagement: Leanpath also fosters a culture of accountability, as employees can see how their actions contribute to reducing waste, encouraging more mindful behaviour.

Practical Tips for Effective Inventory Management and

Waste Reduction

1. Conduct Regular Inventory Audits

Regularly auditing inventory helps identify discrepancies, track stock levels, and prevent overordering. By conducting weekly or monthly audits, businesses can improve accuracy and streamline ordering processes.

2. Involve Staff in Waste Reduction Initiatives

Engaging staff in waste reduction efforts can improve results. Training employees on portion control, waste monitoring, and inventory rotation fosters a shared sense of responsibility and encourages teamwork.

3. Optimize Storage Conditions

Proper storage conditions, such as temperature and humidity control, prolong the freshness of ingredients and reduce spoilage. Storing perishable items in the correct environment ensures that they remain usable for longer.

4. Plan Menus Around Inventory

Menu planning based on available inventory can help minimize waste and streamline operations. Designing menus around ingredients already in stock or incorporating surplus items into specials reduces the need for additional orders.

Building a Sustainable and Efficient Inventory Management System

Effective inventory management and waste reduction

are crucial for a profitable and responsible food business. By tracking stock levels, monitoring waste, and implementing sustainable practices, food entrepreneurs can control costs, reduce environmental impact, and enhance their brand's reputation. As illustrated by examples like Blue Hill, Misfits Market, and Starbucks, sustainable inventory practices align with customer values and contribute to a positive brand image.

By adopting techniques such as portion control, FIFO systems, and cross-utilization of ingredients, food businesses can create an efficient, sustainable inventory system that supports both profitability and customer satisfaction. With the right tools, data, and team engagement, managing inventory and minimizing waste becomes a strategic advantage in the competitive food industry.

CHAPTER 15: HIRING AND TRAINING A STELLAR TEAM

In the food industry, a skilled, motivated team is essential to delivering exceptional customer experiences, maintaining food quality, and ensuring smooth operations. Hiring the right people and investing in comprehensive training are crucial steps for food entrepreneurs looking to build a strong, reliable workforce. Beyond technical skills, qualities like passion, resilience, and a customer-first attitude play a significant role in team dynamics and business success. This chapter explores the key qualities to look for when hiring culinary staff, effective training methods for quality and safety, and real-world examples of food businesses that prioritize team culture and development to drive performance and loyalty.

Qualities to Look for When Hiring Staff for Culinary Roles

Hiring the right team members for a food business goes beyond finding individuals with culinary skills. The ideal candidate possesses a combination of technical expertise, customer service skills, and cultural alignment with the business's values. Here are some essential qualities to consider when hiring for culinary roles.

1. Passion for Food and Hospitality

Passionate employees are more likely to go above and beyond, demonstrating commitment to quality and a positive attitude. Enthusiastic staff members contribute to a vibrant work environment and create memorable experiences for customers. Passionate employees are also more open to learning, improving their skills, and adapting to new challenges.

- Example: Many fine dining restaurants, like Eleven Madison Park in New York, look for candidates who show genuine enthusiasm for culinary arts. Passionate employees contribute to the restaurant's reputation for excellence by consistently delivering high-quality dishes and creating a memorable dining atmosphere.

2. Attention to Detail and Precision

Culinary roles require a high level of attention to detail, from measuring ingredients accurately to plating dishes beautifully. Staff members who demonstrate precision and care in their work are more likely to uphold quality standards and contribute to consistency in every dish.

- Example: In establishments like sushi bars, where the preparation and presentation of each piece require meticulous care, attention to detail is paramount. A sushi chef's ability to deliver perfectly cut fish and precise plating contributes to the overall dining experience.

3. Resilience and Adaptability

The food industry is fast-paced and can be physically demanding. Employees who are resilient and adaptable can handle high-pressure situations, adapt to changing demands, and remain composed during busy shifts. These qualities help ensure smooth operations even during peak hours.

- Example: Food trucks, which often face varying conditions and high customer volumes in short timeframes, rely on staff who are adaptable and able to work efficiently in tight spaces. Resilient employees help maintain service quality regardless of environmental challenges.

4. Strong Customer Service Skills

Customer interactions are an integral part of many culinary roles, particularly in front-of-house positions. Staff members who are friendly, attentive, and empathetic create a welcoming atmosphere that encourages repeat business. In addition, customer-focused employees are more likely to address issues proactively, enhancing the customer experience.

- Example: Chains like Starbucks prioritize customer service in their hiring process, looking for baristas who can engage with customers and foster a positive atmosphere. This focus on customer service has contributed to Starbucks' reputation as a welcoming "third place" where people gather outside of home and work.

5. Teamwork and Communication

Effective teamwork and communication are essential in a kitchen environment, where multiple team members work together to fulfil orders quickly and accurately. Employees who can communicate clearly, cooperate, and support each other help prevent errors, reduce stress, and maintain a productive work environment.

- Example: High-volume kitchens like those at Chipotle rely on teamwork and clear communication to deliver orders quickly and consistently. Each team member's ability to coordinate with others ensures that orders move smoothly through the assembly line, meeting customer expectations for fast service.

Training Methods to Ensure Quality, Customer Service, and Safety

Comprehensive training is essential for building a team that upholds quality, delivers excellent customer service, and adheres to safety standards. Well-designed training programs provide employees with the skills and knowledge needed to excel in their roles, creating a strong foundation for operational success.

1. Onboarding and Orientation

Onboarding introduces new hires to the company's culture, values, and expectations. Effective onboarding fosters a sense of belonging and sets the tone for a positive, supportive work environment.

- Overview of Company Values and Culture: Introduce new employees to the business's mission, vision, and values, explaining how their roles contribute to these goals. This helps create alignment between the employee's responsibilities and the broader purpose of the company.

- Tour of the Facility and Introduction to the Team: Familiarizing new hires with the layout of the kitchen, storage areas, and front-of-house facilities ensures they feel comfortable and prepared. Meeting team members fosters a sense of camaraderie and provides an opportunity to learn from experienced staff.

- Example: Sweetgreen's onboarding process includes an introduction to the company's sustainability mission and the importance of locally sourced ingredients. By connecting employees to the brand's purpose, Sweetgreen fosters a team that feels invested in delivering quality while supporting the environment.

2. Hands-On Training for Technical Skills

Hands-on training is essential for teaching culinary skills, from food preparation and portion control to kitchen equipment usage. In addition, structured, supervised practice allows employees to master techniques and build confidence.

- Shadowing Experienced Team Members: New hires often shadow experienced staff members to learn the ins and outs of their roles. This approach allows them to observe best practices, ask questions, and gradually take on responsibilities under supervision.

- Skill Development and Testing: Practicing specific skills, such as knife techniques or preparing signature dishes, ensures employees can perform their tasks consistently. Skill testing during training helps identify areas for improvement and reinforces quality standards.

- Example: Chipotle's training program includes a structured progression in which new employees learn each step of food preparation and service. Hands-on practice with mentors ensures they can perform tasks efficiently and maintain quality standards.

3. Customer Service Training

Customer service is an essential aspect of many food businesses, particularly those with a strong front-of-house presence. Training employees to interact positively with customers, handle complaints professionally, and foster a welcoming environment enhances the customer experience.

- Empathy and Active Listening: Teaching employees to listen actively and show empathy when addressing customer needs improves interactions and builds trust. Role-playing scenarios can help employees practice responding to different customer situations.

- Complaint Resolution: Training employees in complaint resolution techniques ensures they can handle issues calmly and professionally. This skill is especially important for handling dissatisfied customers, as it can turn a negative experience into a positive one.

- Example: Shake Shack emphasizes "hospitality first" in its customer service training, teaching employees to engage with customers authentically and attentively. This approach reinforces Shake Shack's reputation for friendly service and builds customer loyalty.

4. Health and Safety Training

Health and safety training is essential in any food business, ensuring that employees understand food handling practices, kitchen sanitation, and emergency procedures. Emphasizing safety reduces the risk of foodborne illnesses, accidents, and liability issues.

- Food Safety and Hygiene: Training on proper food storage, temperature control, handwashing, and sanitation practices helps prevent contamination. Regular refreshers reinforce these practices and keep staff updated on any new regulations.
- Equipment Safety: Teaching employees how to safely operate kitchen equipment, including knives, fryers, and ovens, reduces the risk of accidents. Equipment training should also cover maintenance routines to keep tools in good working order.
- Example: Whole Foods provides thorough food safety training for employees, including procedures for handling produce, monitoring temperature, and following cleanliness protocols. This focus on safety ensures that products meet high standards and reduces the risk of contamination.

5. Ongoing Learning and Development

Continuous learning opportunities help employees improve their skills, stay motivated, and advance within the company. Offering cross-training, skill workshops, and leadership development programs demonstrates a commitment to employee growth and enhances team loyalty.

- Cross-Training: Training employees in multiple roles (e.g., both food prep and customer service) increases flexibility, allowing the team to cover shifts or handle peak hours more effectively.

- Skill Workshops and Certifications: Offering workshops on specific skills, such as advanced culinary techniques or barista certifications, helps employees expand their knowledge and feel valued.

- Example: Starbucks provides barista certification and ongoing coffee education, allowing employees to deepen their product knowledge. This investment in training enhances customer service and fosters a sense of pride among staff.

Stories of Food Businesses That Prioritize Team Culture and Development

Successful food businesses recognize that investing in team culture and development pays off in terms of employee retention, customer satisfaction, and brand reputation. Here are some examples of businesses that prioritize team culture to drive long-term success.

1. Union Square Hospitality Group's "Enlightened Hospitality" Approach

Union Square Hospitality Group (USHG), founded by Danny Meyer, is known for its emphasis on "Enlightened Hospitality," a philosophy that values employees as highly as customers. USHG believes that happy employees create a positive atmosphere that enhances the customer experience, leading to long-term loyalty.

- Employee-First Culture: USHG prioritizes team members' well-being, offering competitive wages, benefits, and opportunities for growth. This commitment has resulted in high employee morale and loyalty.

- Ongoing Training and Development: USHG provides continuous training and development, from leadership workshops to customer service skills. This investment in staff has helped the company cultivate a strong, service-focused team that consistently delivers high-quality experiences.

- Example: At USHG's Gramercy Tavern, employees are encouraged to connect with customers personally, creating a warm, welcoming environment. This focus on hospitality has contributed to Gramercy Tavern's reputation as a top dining destination in New York.

2. In-N-Out Burger's Employee Development Program

In-N-Out Burger has built a reputation not only for quality food but also for its employee-centric culture. The company offers its employees competitive pay, a clear career advancement path, and a positive, supportive work environment. This focus on employee satisfaction has helped In-N-Out maintain a dedicated workforce and high service standards.

- Advancement Opportunities: In-N-Out promotes from within, allowing employees to grow into management roles. The clear career path motivates employees to perform well and stay with the company.

- Training and Mentorship: Employees receive hands-on training from experienced mentors who teach the company's values, quality standards, and customer service techniques.

- Example: Many of In-N-Out's store managers started

as entry-level employees, benefiting from the company's development programs. This commitment to employee growth fosters loyalty and ensures that managers are well-versed in In-N-Out's operational standards.

3. Zingerman's Community of Businesses and Staff Empowerment

Zingerman's, a famous deli in Ann Arbor, Michigan, is celebrated for its emphasis on staff empowerment and development. Zingerman's Community of Businesses (ZCoB) is structured as a collaborative group of food-related businesses, each focused on fostering a positive work culture and developing leadership skills among employees.

- Open Book Management: ZCoB uses "open book management," where employees are educated on the business's financials and are encouraged to take ownership of the company's success. This transparency fosters trust and teamwork.
- Employee Training and Growth: Zingerman's offers extensive training in areas like customer service, culinary skills, and business management, creating a well-rounded workforce that feels connected to the brand.

- Example: Zingerman's "ZingTrain" program provides specialized training on customer service, leadership, and business practices. This focus on education and empowerment has contributed to the brand's success and established Zingerman's as a model for positive workplace culture in the food industry.

Building a Strong Team for Lasting Success

Hiring and training a stellar team is essential for creating a successful food business. By focusing on qualities like passion, attention to detail, resilience, customer service, and teamwork, food entrepreneurs can build a team that aligns with their brand values and enhances the customer experience. Comprehensive training in technical skills, customer service, and safety prepares employees to meet operational standards and handle challenges effectively.

As illustrated by businesses like Union Square Hospitality Group, In-N-Out Burger, and Zingerman's, investing in team culture and development pays off in terms of employee retention, customer satisfaction, and brand reputation. Prioritizing team-building, professional growth, and a positive work environment creates a loyal, motivated workforce that drives long-term success.

CHAPTER 16: BUILDING A BRAND IN THE FOOD INDUSTRY

In the competitive landscape of the food industry, a strong brand is more than just a name or logo; it is the essence that defines a business, connects with customers on an emotional level, and fosters loyalty. A brand's identity communicates its values, mission, and unique story, setting it apart from the competition and attracting a dedicated customer base. This chapter explores the essential elements of brand identity, the impact of brand values on customer loyalty, and case studies of successful culinary brands that have leveraged branding strategies to make a lasting impact in the industry.

Elements of Brand Identity: Name, Logo, Ambiance, and Storytelling

Building a compelling brand identity requires thoughtful

consideration of each element that will shape how customers perceive the business. From the name and logo to the ambiance and storytelling, every detail contributes to a cohesive brand image that resonates with customers and creates memorable experiences.

1. Brand Name and Logo

The brand name and logo are the first elements that customers encounter, often forming the basis of their first impression. An effective name and logo reflect the brand's personality, hint at its offerings, and make a memorable impact. In the food industry, where competition is high, a distinctive name and logo can capture attention and help customers remember the business.

- Naming Considerations: A great name is easy to pronounce, memorable, and relevant to the brand's concept. Whether playful, refined, or straightforward, the name should align with the business's tone and target audience.

- Logo Design: A logo visually represents the brand and should be simple, versatile, and consistent with the brand's values. Many food businesses opt for logos that include visual cues about their cuisine or dining style, such as a spoon, fork, or coffee cup.

- Example: The name "Shake Shack" is playful and catchy, reflecting a casual, accessible dining experience. The logo, featuring a stylized burger, instantly communicates the type of food served and resonates with a broad audience.

2. Ambiance and Interior Design

The physical space where customers interact with the brand plays a significant role in shaping their perception. Ambiance, decor, lighting, music, and layout collectively create the atmosphere that defines the dining experience and reinforces the brand's identity.

- Decor and Design: Interior design choices, from furniture to colour schemes, should reflect the brand's style and theme. A rustic, farm-to-table restaurant might use natural materials and warm lighting, while a modern, fast-casual eatery might opt for minimalist decor and bright colours.

- Consistency with Brand Values: The ambiance should align with the brand's mission and values. For example, a health-focused brand might use eco-friendly decor, emphasizing its commitment to sustainability.

- Example: Starbucks creates a consistent, cozy atmosphere across all locations, with soft lighting, comfortable seating, and a mix of wood and earth tones. This ambiance makes Starbucks a welcoming "third place" where people feel comfortable working, socializing, or relaxing.

3. Storytelling

Storytelling is a powerful branding tool that connects customers to the brand's mission, values, and origins. A compelling brand story creates an emotional connection, making customers feel invested in the brand's journey and purpose.

- Brand Origin and Purpose: Sharing the story behind the brand's creation, such as the founder's inspiration or a personal mission, humanizes the business and builds trust.

- Community and Impact: Highlighting the brand's positive impact, whether through local sourcing, charitable partnerships, or sustainability efforts, can inspire loyalty among customers who share those values.

- Example: Ben & Jerry's shares the story of its humble beginnings in a converted gas station, emphasizing the founders' commitment to quality, sustainability, and social justice. This narrative resonates with customers who appreciate the brand's ethical values and authentic approach.

How Brand Values and Mission Influence Customer Loyalty

A brand's values and mission shape its identity and influence how customers perceive and connect with it. Customers are increasingly drawn to brands that align with their own values and stand for a cause beyond profit. In the food industry, where consumers care about health, sustainability, and social responsibility, a strong mission can inspire loyalty and create lifelong customers.

1. Building Emotional Connections Through Values

Customers are more likely to support brands that reflect their values, whether that's promoting sustainability, supporting local communities, or offering ethically sourced ingredients. By clearly communicating these values, brands can foster emotional connections that go beyond the product.

- Transparency and Authenticity: Customers appreciate brands that are open about their sourcing, ingredients, and business practices. Transparent communication builds trust and reinforces the brand's integrity.

- Aligning with Customer Values: Brands that align with customers' personal beliefs and lifestyle choices can build stronger, more loyal customer bases. For instance, vegan or organic brands attract health-conscious consumers who value clean eating.

- Example: Chipotle's commitment to "Food with Integrity" emphasizes responsibly sourced ingredients, such as organic produce and antibiotic-free meat. This mission resonates with customers who prioritize ethical dining options, resulting in a loyal customer base.

2. Creating a Sense of Community

A strong brand doesn't just attract customers; it builds a community around shared values and experiences. By fostering a sense of belonging and inclusivity, brands can create an environment where customers feel part of something meaningful.

- Engagement and Interaction: Engaging customers through social media, events, and loyalty programs helps build a community and encourages repeat visits.

- Personalization: Brands that offer personalized experiences, whether through customized menu items or tailored loyalty rewards, show that they value their customers as individuals, strengthening brand loyalty.

- Example: Sweetgreen's "Sweetgreen in Schools" program educates children about healthy eating and sustainability. By engaging the community and promoting shared values, Sweetgreen builds a loyal following of health-conscious customers who appreciate the brand's commitment to education and well-being.

3. Differentiation Through Mission-Driven Branding

In a crowded market, a strong mission sets a brand apart from competitors. Mission-driven branding highlights what makes the brand unique and reinforces its purpose, giving customers a reason to choose it over others.

- Standing for a Cause: Many successful food brands are associated with a specific cause, such as environmental conservation, fair trade, or animal welfare. Customers who support these causes often choose to support the brand as well.
- Consistent Messaging: A clear, consistent message about the brand's mission resonates with customers and reinforces the brand's identity. Consistency across marketing materials, social media, and in-store displays solidifies the brand's values in the customer's mind.
- Example: The Body Shop, though not a food brand, provides an excellent example of mission-driven branding by advocating for cruelty-free products and ethical sourcing. This strong, consistent mission has helped it differentiate itself from other beauty brands, creating a loyal customer base that aligns with its values.

Case Studies of Strong Culinary Brands and Their Branding Strategies

Examining the branding strategies of successful culinary brands provides valuable insights into how each element of brand identity, values, and mission contributes to long-term success.

1. Shake Shack: The Power of Simple, Transparent Branding

Shake Shack started as a hot dog cart in New York City's Madison Square Park and has since become a globally recognized brand known for its high-quality burgers and milkshakes. Its success lies in its simplicity, transparency, and commitment to quality.

- Consistency Across Locations: Shake Shack maintains a consistent brand identity across all locations, with a minimalist design and a straightforward menu that highlights high-quality ingredients. The consistent experience makes Shake Shack recognizable and reliable, regardless of location.
- Focus on Quality Ingredients: The brand emphasizes its use of hormone-free meat, fresh ingredients, and eco-friendly packaging, appealing to customers who prioritize quality and sustainability.
- Community Engagement: Shake Shack frequently partners with local businesses and chefs to create location-specific menu items, fostering a sense of community and supporting local talent.

Shake Shack's transparent, quality-focused branding has helped it build a strong reputation and a loyal customer base that values its straightforward approach to fast-casual dining.

2. Ben & Jerry's: Social Responsibility as a Brand Identity

Ben & Jerry's has built a global reputation not only for its creative ice cream flavours but also for its commitment to social and environmental causes. Its brand identity is closely tied to its mission of promoting social justice, environmental sustainability, and ethical business practices.

- Activism and Social Impact: Ben & Jerry's actively supports causes like climate change, marriage equality, and racial justice, reinforcing its image as a socially responsible brand. Its activism resonates with customers who share similar values, creating a strong sense of loyalty and support.

- Brand Story and Transparency: The company's story, from a small scoop shop in Vermont to an internationally recognized brand, adds authenticity and appeal. Ben & Jerry's is transparent about its sourcing and ingredients, which builds trust with customers.

- Engaging Marketing Campaigns: Ben & Jerry's marketing campaigns often promote its social mission, using social media and unique flavours (like "Justice ReMix'd") to spread awareness and engage with customers.

By incorporating social responsibility into every aspect of its brand, Ben & Jerry's has created a powerful, values-driven identity that resonates deeply with customers who prioritize ethical brands.

3. In-N-Out Burger: Family-Owned, Quality-Focused Brand Legacy

In-N-Out Burger, a family-owned burger chain, has established a dedicated customer following due to its unwavering focus on quality, consistency, and a strong family-centred brand identity. Despite its growth, the brand remains true to its core values, which has fostered a loyal fan base.

- Consistency and Quality: In-N-Out maintains strict quality standards, using fresh ingredients and preparing food to order. Its commitment to quality has built trust with customers who know they can expect the same experience at any location.

- Limited Menu: The brand's limited menu, featuring burgers, fries, and shakes, keeps the focus on quality and simplicity, allowing In-N-Out to master each item. The simplicity of the menu reinforces its identity as a classic, no-frills burger chain.

- Cult Following and Nostalgia: In-N-Out's old-school aesthetic, paper hats, and retro logo contribute to its nostalgic appeal. The brand's customer-first approach and family-centred culture have also helped it build a dedicated fan base that sees In-N-Out as more than just a burger joint.

In-N-Out's emphasis on quality, consistency, and family values has resulted in a brand legacy that attracts loyal customers and stands out in the fast-food industry.

Crafting a Strong Brand in the Food Industry

Building a successful brand in the food industry involves more than designing a logo or choosing a catchy name. A strong brand reflects its values, mission, and identity in every aspect, from the ambiance and menu to customer interactions and marketing campaigns. By emphasizing authenticity, transparency, and consistency, food entrepreneurs can create brands that resonate with their target audience, foster loyalty, and stand out in a competitive market.

The case studies of Shake Shack, Ben & Jerry's, and In-N-Out Burger illustrate how brands can successfully leverage different aspects of branding, from simplicity and quality to social responsibility and nostalgia, to create strong, memorable identities. By focusing on core values and building a cohesive brand experience, food businesses can cultivate loyal customer bases and achieve long-term success.

CHAPTER 17: DIGITAL MARKETING FOR CULINARY VENTURES

In today's digital landscape, a strong online presence is essential for culinary businesses to reach their target audience, engage with customers, and drive growth. Digital marketing, encompassing social media, website optimization, and online reviews, plays a pivotal role in shaping a brand's identity and building customer loyalty. For food businesses, platforms like Instagram, Facebook, and TikTok offer dynamic opportunities to showcase offerings visually, connect with followers, and cultivate a loyal fanbase. This chapter will cover strategies for leveraging digital platforms, creating engaging content, and explore real-life examples of food brands that excel in digital marketing.

Leveraging Social Media, Website SEO, and Online Reviews

1. Social Media Marketing

Social media platforms are powerful tools for building brand awareness, engaging with customers, and showcasing a business's unique offerings. Each platform serves a distinct purpose, allowing businesses to connect with various audiences in creative ways.

- Instagram: Known for its visual appeal, Instagram is ideal for food businesses to share high-quality photos and videos of dishes, behind-the-scenes moments, and user-generated content. With features like Stories and Reels, businesses can engage followers through interactive content.

- Facebook: Facebook is useful for sharing long-form content, such as event announcements, blogs, and customer reviews. Its advertising capabilities allow businesses to reach specific demographics based on location, age, and interests.

- TikTok: With its focus on short, engaging videos, TikTok is popular among younger audiences. Food brands use TikTok to showcase recipes, food hacks, and viral challenges, creating a sense of authenticity and spontaneity that resonates with viewers.

- Example: Starbucks effectively uses Instagram to post visually stunning images of seasonal drinks, desserts, and themed campaigns. The brand's engaging, on-trend content keeps followers excited about new offerings and promotes a sense of community among coffee lovers.

2. Website SEO (Search Engine Optimization)

An optimized website helps food businesses attract customers by making it easy for them to find the business online. SEO involves enhancing website content and structure so it ranks higher in search engine results, increasing visibility for potential customers.

- Keyword Optimization: Using relevant keywords (e.g., "best Italian restaurant in [city]" or "organic coffee shop") throughout the website's content, titles, and meta descriptions improves search rankings.
- Mobile Optimization: Many customers search for restaurants on their phones, making mobile-friendly design essential. Ensuring the site loads quickly, has easy navigation, and offers click-to-call or map features enhances the user experience.
- Local SEO: Registering the business with Google My Business, Bing Places, and Yelp helps attract local customers. These listings often appear in local search results, especially for customers searching for "nearby" or "open now" options.
- Example: Sweetgreen's website is optimized for both SEO and mobile, with an easy-to-navigate layout and clear descriptions of its healthy food offerings. The site also includes a location finder, making it easy for health-conscious customers to locate the nearest Sweetgreen restaurant.

3. Online Reviews and Reputation Management

Positive online reviews build trust with potential customers, while negative reviews offer opportunities to show responsiveness and commitment to customer satisfaction. Actively managing online reviews on platforms like Yelp, Google Reviews, and TripAdvisor enhances brand reputation and drives customer engagement.

- Encouraging Reviews: Asking satisfied customers to leave reviews on platforms like Yelp or Google helps build a collection of positive testimonials. Some businesses encourage reviews by offering incentives, such as discounts or loyalty points.

- Responding to Reviews: Responding professionally to both positive and negative reviews demonstrates customer care. Addressing complaints respectfully and offering solutions shows potential customers that the business values feedback.

- Example: Chipotle actively monitors and responds to customer feedback on social media and review sites. The brand's quick, courteous responses to customer concerns and praise for positive feedback help maintain its customer-centric reputation.

Creating Engaging Content for Platforms Like Instagram, Facebook, and TikTok

Effective content captures attention, encourages interaction, and keeps followers returning for more. For food brands, visually appealing content showcasing delicious dishes, behind-the-scenes action, and customer experiences can inspire engagement and build loyalty.

1. Visual Storytelling on Instagram

Instagram's focus on visuals makes it a perfect platform for food brands to showcase their creations.

High-quality images and videos, combined with creative captions, can convey the brand's story, values, and personality.

- Food Photography: Lighting, composition, and angles are essential for mouth-watering food photography. Images should highlight the texture, colour, and plating of dishes to make them look irresistible.

- User-Generated Content (UGC): Encouraging customers to share their photos and tag the brand creates a sense of community. Sharing UGC on the brand's feed and stories not only adds authenticity but also strengthens customer relationships.

- Example: Jeni's Splendid Ice Creams shares beautifully shot images of its unique ice cream flavours on Instagram. The brand also reposts UGC, featuring customers enjoying their ice cream, creating a fun, community-driven atmosphere.

2. Behind-the-Scenes Content on Facebook

Facebook allows for a variety of content types, from images and videos to articles and event updates. Behind-the-scenes content, such as chef spotlights, kitchen processes, or ingredient sourcing stories, gives customers an insider's view into the brand's operations and builds transparency.

- Chef Spotlights and Employee Stories: Highlighting team members adds a personal touch and builds emotional connections. Sharing short stories about chefs, employees, or suppliers shows the people behind the brand.

- Event Announcements and Special Offers: Facebook

is ideal for announcing events, promotions, or seasonal menus. Food businesses can use Facebook Events to invite customers to special tasting nights, cooking classes, or community events.

- Example: Panera Bread frequently posts behind-the-scenes content, showcasing its sourcing of fresh ingredients and profiles of its employees. These posts align with Panera's brand values and reinforce its commitment to quality and transparency.

3. Trending Challenges and Viral Content on TikTok

TikTok's video format and emphasis on trends make it an ideal platform for food brands to reach a young, engaged audience. Brands can participate in trending challenges, share fun food hacks, or showcase unique recipes that viewers can try at home.

- Challenges and Hashtags: Engaging with popular challenges, such as recipe or "behind-the-scenes" trends, can attract more followers. Brands can also create their own challenges, inviting customers to participate and share their content with branded hashtags.

- Recipe Demonstrations and Food Hacks: Short, snappy videos demonstrating recipes or food hacks attract viewers and encourage them to share the content. By showcasing signature dishes, brands can also inspire customers to visit or order online.

- Example: Dunkin' has excelled on TikTok by participating in trends and collaborating with popular influencers, such as Charli D'Amelio. Dunkin's content often includes drink recipes and promotions related to TikTok trends, keeping the brand relevant to young audiences.

Real-Life Examples of Food Brands that Excel at Digital Marketing

Several food brands have used digital marketing to strengthen their brand identity, engage customers, and drive growth. Here are three examples of brands that excel at digital marketing and the strategies that have made them successful.

1. Domino's Pizza: Multi-Platform Engagement and User-Centric Campaigns

Domino's Pizza has successfully integrated digital marketing into its business model, creating an engaging and user-friendly online presence. Its approach to digital marketing focuses on multi-platform engagement and user-centric innovations.

- Interactive Campaigns: Domino's "Tweet-to-Order" campaign allowed customers to order pizza by tweeting a pizza emoji to the Domino's Twitter account. This creative approach simplified the ordering process and created buzz around the brand.

- Innovative Ordering Options: Domino's has invested heavily in digital innovations, such as its mobile app and voice-activated ordering. By focusing on customer convenience, Domino's attracts a tech-savvy audience that values streamlined ordering options.

- Consistent Engagement Across Platforms: Domino's is active on multiple social media platforms, including Instagram, Twitter, and Facebook. Its humorous, customer-focused posts build a relatable brand image that resonates with followers.

Domino's digital-first approach and focus on user-friendly technology have helped it become a leader in the competitive pizza market, illustrating how digital engagement can elevate a brand's appeal.

2. Wendy's: Bold and Interactive Social Media Presence

Wendy's has gained a reputation for its bold, witty social media personality, especially on Twitter, where it interacts with followers, competitors, and even memes in humorous, memorable ways. Wendy's approach to digital marketing demonstrates how a distinct, playful tone can set a brand apart.

- Witty, Bold Brand Voice: Wendy's Twitter account is known for its snarky responses, roasts, and humorous interactions with followers. This voice appeals to a younger audience and creates a brand personality that's engaging and entertaining.
- Social Media Campaigns: Wendy's runs creative campaigns, such as "NationalRoastDay," where followers ask Wendy's to "roast" them. These campaigns encourage user interaction and create a buzz around the brand.
- Engagement with Trends: Wendy's is quick to participate in trending memes, challenges, and conversations, keeping its content fresh and relevant. This real-time engagement strengthens Wendy's connection with its audience and boosts brand visibility.

Wendy's has turned its social media presence into a competitive advantage, using humour and wit to differentiate itself and engage with a wide audience, making it one of the most recognized fast-food brands on social media.

3. Chipotle: Innovative Content and Customer Engagement

Chipotle has successfully leveraged social media to showcase its commitment to quality ingredients, sustainability, and transparency. Its digital marketing strategy emphasizes storytelling and interactive content that resonates with its health-conscious, eco-aware audience.

- Transparency and Authenticity: Chipotle uses digital platforms to educate customers about its ingredients, sourcing practices, and sustainability initiatives. This transparency builds trust and aligns with customer values.

- Interactive Content and Challenges: On TikTok, Chipotle has created popular challenges, such as the "Chipotle Lid Flip Challenge," that encourage followers to participate and share their own content. By fostering engagement, Chipotle strengthens its community and extends its reach.

- UGC and Influencer Collaborations: Chipotle often shares user-generated content and collaborates with influencers to reach new audiences. These collaborations increase credibility and drive awareness among followers.

Chipotle's focus on transparency, engagement, and customer participation has allowed it to cultivate a loyal following and reinforce its brand identity as a socially responsible, quality-focused food brand.

Building a Strong Digital Marketing Presence

For food businesses, a well-crafted digital marketing strategy is essential for reaching and engaging customers in today's digital age. By leveraging social media, SEO, and online reviews, food brands can connect with their target audience, strengthen their brand identity, and foster customer loyalty. Through engaging content, consistent brand voice, and responsive online interactions, businesses can create memorable digital experiences that drive growth and establish a loyal customer base.

As demonstrated by Domino's, Wendy's, and Chipotle, success in digital marketing comes from understanding the audience, adapting to trends, and creating engaging, authentic content. By adopting similar strategies and focusing on customer engagement, food entrepreneurs can harness the power of digital platforms to build a strong, enduring brand.

CHAPTER 18: CUSTOMER EXPERIENCE AND RELATIONSHIP MANAGEMENT

Exceptional customer service is at the heart of every successful food business. It's not just about serving good food; it's about creating memorable experiences that make customers feel valued and eager to return. Building strong relationships with customers fosters loyalty, drives positive word-of-mouth, and contributes to long-term success. This chapter explores the importance of exceptional customer service, techniques for gathering and responding to customer feedback, and showcases success stories of food businesses with loyal customer bases built on strong relationships.

The Importance of Exceptional Customer Service in Food Businesses

Customer service is a critical component of the dining experience, influencing everything from first impressions to repeat visits. Exceptional customer service not only enhances the overall experience but also differentiates a brand in a competitive market. For many customers, positive interactions with staff, timely service, and attentive care can be as important as the food itself.

1. Creating a Welcoming Atmosphere

A warm, inviting environment sets the tone for the customer experience. From greeting customers upon arrival to providing attentive service throughout their visit, every interaction contributes to how the brand is perceived.

- First Impressions: The initial greeting from the host, server, or cashier has a lasting impact. Friendly, prompt service helps customers feel comfortable and valued from the start.

- Attentive Service: Checking on customers during their meal, addressing any issues, and responding to special requests with enthusiasm demonstrates attentiveness and respect for customer needs.

- Example: Chick-fil-A is renowned for its customer-centric approach, where employees are trained to provide consistently polite and friendly service, often ending interactions with "my pleasure." This attention to customer experience has fostered a loyal customer base and set Chick-fil-A apart in the fast-food industry.

2. Building Emotional Connections

Building emotional connections with customers creates a sense of belonging, transforming one-time customers into loyal regulars. Small gestures, like remembering a customer's name or favourite order, make customers feel recognized and appreciated.

- Personalized Interactions: Personalized service, such as customizing orders or remembering preferences, adds a personal touch that makes customers feel valued.

- Empathy and Understanding: Listening to customers, addressing their concerns, and handling complaints with empathy demonstrate that the business values customer satisfaction.

- Example: Starbucks baristas often remember regular customers' orders and names, making the coffee chain feel more personal and community-oriented. This personalized approach has strengthened Starbucks' brand and customer loyalty worldwide.

3. Creating Consistency Across All Touchpoints

Consistency in service quality ensures that customers have a reliable experience every time they visit. From the quality of food to the friendliness of staff, maintaining high standards builds trust and encourages repeat visits.

- Standardized Training: Training staff to deliver consistent service across all locations ensures that customers know what to expect, no matter where they are.

- Uniform Service Policies: Establishing service protocols, such as response times and complaint resolution, creates uniformity in how customers are treated.

- Example: The Cheesecake Factory is known for its extensive staff training and consistent quality across locations. From wait times to food quality, customers can expect a similar experience at any Cheesecake Factory restaurant, contributing to a loyal customer base.

Techniques for Gathering Customer Feedback and Implementing Improvements

Gathering customer feedback is essential for understanding customer needs, identifying areas for improvement, and continuously enhancing the dining experience. By actively seeking feedback and implementing changes based on customer insights, food businesses can foster loyalty and improve satisfaction.

1. Surveys and Feedback Forms

Surveys and feedback forms provide structured opportunities for customers to share their thoughts. These tools can be distributed via email, displayed on receipts, or provided digitally through QR codes at the table or counter.

- Post-Visit Surveys: Sending follow-up emails with survey links allows customers to provide feedback after their visit. Post-visit surveys help businesses gather insights on food quality, service, and ambiance.
- In-House Feedback Forms: Offering feedback forms at the restaurant gives customers a chance to share their thoughts immediately. Forms should be simple, with space for both ratings and open-ended comments.
- Example: Olive Garden includes a survey link on

its receipts, encouraging customers to share feedback on their dining experience. The survey results provide insights that the restaurant can use to refine service and improve customer satisfaction.

2. Social Media Monitoring

Social media platforms provide a wealth of customer feedback, both positive and negative. Monitoring social media allows businesses to see what customers are saying about their brand, identify trends, and respond to feedback publicly.

- Engaging with Comments and Reviews: Responding to comments on social media shows customers that the business values their opinions. Thanking customers for positive feedback and addressing complaints demonstrates responsiveness.

- Tracking Sentiment: Using social media analytics tools to track sentiment and identify recurring themes in customer feedback can help businesses proactively address issues.

- Example: Wendy's uses Twitter to engage with customers, responding to compliments and complaints alike. This active engagement helps Wendy's build a community and foster brand loyalty among social media followers.

3. Online Reviews and Third-Party Platforms

Reviews on sites like Yelp, Google, and TripAdvisor influence prospective customers and shape brand reputation. Proactively managing these reviews and responding to both positive and negative feedback can significantly impact a business's image.

- Encouraging Positive Reviews: Inviting satisfied customers to leave reviews on platforms like Google or Yelp helps boost the brand's online reputation.

- Addressing Negative Reviews: Responding to negative reviews with empathy and offering solutions, such as inviting the customer back for a second try, demonstrates a commitment to customer satisfaction.

- Example: Chipotle actively monitors and responds to reviews on Google and Yelp, addressing complaints and thanking customers for positive feedback. This responsiveness shows that Chipotle values its customers' experiences and strives for continuous improvement.

4. Feedback Collection at Point of Sale

Collecting feedback at the point of sale (POS) enables businesses to gather immediate insights directly from customers. POS feedback can be as simple as a short survey on the receipt or a digital rating prompt on a tablet at checkout.

- Tablet-Based Ratings: Digital ratings allow customers to provide quick feedback on their experience by tapping a smiley or frown face before they leave.

- Incentivized Surveys: Offering a small discount or reward for completing a survey incentivizes customers to share feedback and provides the business with valuable insights.

- Example: McDonald's uses kiosks with survey prompts, asking customers to rate their satisfaction with the visit. These instant feedback options provide real-time data that the company can use to address any immediate concerns.

5. Incorporating Feedback into Improvement Initiatives

Collecting feedback is only the first step; it's equally important to implement improvements based on customer insights. By actively addressing customer feedback, businesses demonstrate their commitment to enhancing the customer experience.

- Analysing Patterns: Reviewing feedback regularly to identify recurring issues, such as slow service or menu limitations, helps businesses address root causes and make meaningful changes.

- Training Adjustments: If feedback indicates a need for improvement in specific areas, such as customer service or food presentation, targeted training sessions can help staff meet expectations.

- Example: Panera Bread periodically updates its menu based on customer feedback, offering new items or improving existing ones. By listening to customer preferences, Panera adapts its offerings to better align with customer tastes.

Success Stories of Businesses with Loyal Customer Bases

Several food businesses have earned loyal customer bases by prioritizing exceptional customer experience and relationship management. Here are some examples of brands that have successfully fostered loyalty through customer-centric practices.

1. Trader Joe's: Exceptional Customer Engagement and Store Experience

Trader Joe's, a popular grocery store chain, is known for

its unique products, friendly staff, and welcoming store atmosphere. By focusing on customer experience, Trader Joe's has cultivated a loyal customer base that values its approachable, personable approach.

- Friendly Staff and Customer Engagement: Trader Joe's employees are encouraged to engage with customers, help, and provide product recommendations. This focus on personal interaction makes shopping at Trader Joe's feel more like a friendly neighbourhood experience.

- Responsive to Feedback: Trader Joe's listens to customer feedback when selecting and introducing new products. Seasonal items and limited-time offerings are often a result of customer demand, making shoppers feel valued and heard.

- Impact: Trader Joe's loyal customers appreciate the store's personal touch, unique product selection, and responsiveness to feedback, making it one of the most beloved grocery chains in the U.S.

2. In-N-Out Burger: Consistent Quality and Customer-First Culture

In-N-Out Burger has a dedicated following thanks to its commitment to quality, customer-centric culture, and consistent experience across all locations. Known for its simple menu and focus on fresh ingredients, In-N-Out has built a brand that customers trust and admire.

- Consistency and Quality Standards: In-N-Out maintains strict quality standards, from ingredient sourcing to preparation. Customers know that every visit will offer the same level of quality, reinforcing brand loyalty.

- Personalized Service and Customer Care: In-N-Out employees are trained to provide warm, friendly service. This personalized care, combined with quality food, has helped the brand build a customer base that feels valued and respected.

- Impact: In-N-Out's emphasis on consistent quality and positive customer interactions has fostered a strong, loyal following that continues to support the brand passionately.

3. Zappos: Legendary Customer Service and Relationship Building

While not a food business, Zappos' legendary customer service provides valuable lessons for the food industry. The online shoe retailer has earned a reputation for going above and beyond to make customers happy

, which has led to a loyal, passionate customer base.

- Customer-Centric Service Philosophy: Zappos' commitment to exceptional service includes a 24/7 customer service hotline, generous return policies, and a philosophy that empowers employees to make customers happy at any cost.
- Building Relationships Through Service: Zappos sees every customer interaction as an opportunity to build a lasting relationship. Employees are encouraged to personalize interactions, even if it means spending extra time with a customer.

- Impact: Zappos' dedication to customer service has led to a fiercely loyal customer base and numerous stories of extraordinary service that have strengthened its brand reputation.

- Lesson for Food Businesses: Zappos' approach to customer service demonstrates the importance of building relationships over simply making sales. Food businesses that prioritize customer happiness and view service as relationship-building can create similar loyalty.

Fostering Loyalty Through Exceptional Customer Experience

Delivering an exceptional customer experience is essential for food businesses seeking to build loyalty and differentiate themselves in a competitive market. From providing friendly, personalized service to gathering and responding to feedback, every aspect of the customer journey contributes to a positive brand image and repeat business.

As shown in the success stories of Trader Joe's, In-N-Out Burger, and Zappos, focusing on consistency, quality, and personalized care cultivates loyal customers who return time and again. By prioritizing customer satisfaction and relationship management, food businesses can build strong, lasting connections that drive growth and support long-term success.

CHAPTER 19: MANAGING REPUTATION AND CRISIS COMMUNICATIONS

In the fast-paced and highly competitive food industry, reputation is everything. A single negative incident or poorly handled customer complaint can damage a brand's public image, especially in the age of social media, where news travels rapidly. For food businesses, knowing how to manage reputation and handle crises with transparency and grace is essential for maintaining customer trust and loyalty. This chapter explores strategies for handling negative reviews and public relations (PR) crises, methods for building trust with customers during challenging times, and real-life examples of food brands that effectively managed crises to emerge stronger.

Strategies for Handling Negative Reviews and PR Crises

Negative reviews and PR crises are inevitable in the food industry. Whether it's a critical online review or a larger crisis, such as a food safety issue, how a business responds can significantly impact its reputation. With a proactive approach and thoughtful response strategies, food businesses can mitigate damage and even improve customer loyalty.

1. Responding to Negative Reviews with Professionalism and Empathy

Online reviews have a strong influence on customer perceptions, and negative reviews are often the most visible. Responding to these reviews with professionalism and empathy demonstrates that the business values feedback and is committed to improvement.

- Acknowledging the Customer's Experience: Start by acknowledging the customer's perspective and empathizing with their dissatisfaction. Avoid defensiveness and focus on making the customer feel heard.

- Offering a Resolution: Address the issue directly and offer a solution, such as a replacement meal, refund, or invitation to return. By taking proactive steps to make things right, the business shows commitment to customer satisfaction.

- Encouraging Direct Communication: Invite the customer to discuss their experience further by providing a contact number or email. This private approach allows for a more personalized resolution and reduces the likelihood of a public back-and-forth.

- Example: Shake Shack is known for responding to negative reviews with professionalism. When customers raise concerns, Shake Shack's representatives acknowledge the feedback, apologize for any shortcomings, and offer ways to resolve the issue, whether by inviting the customer back or addressing the specific complaint.

2. Developing a Crisis Communication Plan

A crisis communication plan is essential for any food business, as it prepares the team to respond swiftly and effectively in the event of a PR crisis. This plan outlines steps to address potential issues, from foodborne illnesses to negative press coverage, and ensures the business is ready to respond.

- Identify Key Personnel and Spokespeople: Designate specific team members responsible for handling media inquiries and communicating with the public. Having trained spokespeople helps ensure a consistent message.
- Craft Key Messaging: Develop core messages that align with the brand's values and address the crisis directly. These messages should be clear, empathetic, and informative, helping to calm concerns and build trust.
- Establish Communication Channels: Determine which channels to use for different types of crises. Social media is often the first point of contact for public statements, while more serious issues may require press releases or media interviews.

- Example: When Chipotle faced a food safety crisis

in 2015 due to an E. coli outbreak, the company had to quickly communicate with the public. Chipotle issued public apologies, suspended operations at affected locations, and communicated frequently with customers and media to keep the public informed about ongoing safety measures.

3. Monitoring Social Media and Public Sentiment

Social media plays a significant role in shaping public perception, especially during crises. Monitoring online sentiment helps businesses stay informed about what customers are saying, respond to emerging issues quickly, and adjust messaging as needed.

- Use Social Listening Tools: Tools like Hootsuite, Sprout Social, and Brandwatch allow businesses to monitor mentions of their brand and track changes in sentiment. These tools alert businesses to trending issues before they escalate.

- Engage Proactively: Engaging with customers proactively, whether through regular posts or responses to questions, shows transparency and builds trust. During a crisis, proactive engagement helps the business control the narrative and keep customers informed.

- Example: Wendy's actively monitors social media and engages with customers during controversies or PR challenges. By responding with humour, honesty, and empathy, Wendy's often turns challenging situations into opportunities to reinforce its bold brand personality and transparency.

4. Owning Up to Mistakes and Showing Accountability

Honesty and accountability are crucial during any

crisis. When a business acknowledges its mistakes, explains the steps it's taking to rectify the issue, and demonstrates a commitment to improvement, it rebuilds trust with customers and minimizes reputational damage.

- Apologize and Take Responsibility: A genuine apology, without deflection or blame-shifting, shows respect for customers' concerns. Taking responsibility is especially important if the issue is a result of a mistake on the business's part.

- Outline Steps for Improvement: Explaining how the business plans to prevent similar incidents reassures customers and highlights the company's commitment to high standards.

- Follow Up: After the initial response, following up with updates on improvements or policy changes demonstrates accountability and a genuine interest in preventing future issues.

- Example: In 2018, Starbucks faced backlash after a controversial incident in one of its stores. The company quickly apologized, took responsibility, and closed stores nationwide for a day to provide racial bias training for employees. This response showed accountability and a commitment to addressing the issue, helping Starbucks repair its image.

Building Trust and Transparency with Customers During Crises

Transparency and trust are essential for maintaining customer loyalty, especially during challenging times. Customers value honesty and are more likely to forgive a brand that communicates openly and addresses issues responsibly.

1. Maintaining Open Communication

Open, honest communication is critical during a crisis. Regular updates on the situation, shared through multiple channels, help alleviate customer concerns and build confidence that the business is managing the issue effectively.

- Timely Updates: Providing timely updates keeps customers informed and reassured. Updates should be concise, fact-based, and free of unnecessary jargon.

- Multiple Communication Channels: Use a mix of channels, such as social media, email newsletters, and website updates, to reach customers where they are most active. Consistency across these channels ensures that customers receive the same message.

- Example: In 2017, McDonald's faced an issue with contaminated lettuce in some locations. The company communicated openly, providing regular updates on affected locations and detailing the steps it was taking to ensure food safety. This transparency helped maintain customer trust and mitigated potential reputational damage.

2. Prioritizing Customer Safety and Well-Being

During a crisis, prioritizing customer safety above all else reinforces the brand's commitment to customer care. Actions like halting production, issuing recalls, or offering refunds show that the business values safety and customer well-being over profit.

- Product Recalls and Refunds: If an issue affects product safety, issuing a recall or offering refunds demonstrates responsibility and protects customers.

- Preventative Measures: Explaining the steps taken to prevent similar incidents in the future reassures customers that their safety is a priority.

- Example: Blue Bell Creameries issued a voluntary recall of its ice cream products after a listeria outbreak. The company took immediate action to remove products from stores, apologized to customers, and overhauled its safety protocols to prevent recurrence. This response showed a clear commitment to customer safety and helped Blue Bell rebuild trust with its loyal customer base.

3. Engaging with Media Responsibly

Managing relationships with the media is essential during a crisis. Providing accurate information, designating trained spokespeople, and responding to media inquiries promptly helps maintain control over the brand's narrative and prevents misinformation.

- Prepare Spokespeople: Trained spokespeople who understand the brand's messaging and crisis response strategy can communicate effectively with the media, reducing the risk of misunderstandings.

- Stay Calm and Consistent: Maintaining a calm, factual tone in media statements helps control the narrative and prevents the situation from escalating.

- Example: When facing public scrutiny, Chipotle's spokespeople communicated openly with the media, explaining the brand's food safety improvements and responding to inquiries. This consistent messaging demonstrated Chipotle's dedication to transparency and helped restore public trust.

4. Turning the Crisis into a Learning Opportunity

Some brands emerge from crises stronger by using the experience as a catalyst for positive change. When a business acknowledges shortcomings, makes improvements, and educates customers about these changes, it often rebuilds trust and strengthens loyalty.

- Publicly Share Improvements: Sharing updates about new policies, training programs, or safety measures shows that the brand is learning from the incident and taking meaningful action.
- Commit to Ongoing Improvement: Communicating a long-term commitment to quality and accountability reinforces that the business is continuously striving to do better.
- Example: After implementing new food safety protocols, Chipotle shared these improvements publicly, explaining its efforts to exceed industry standards. By framing the crisis as a turning point, Chipotle regained customer trust and improved its brand reputation.

Examples of Food Businesses that Effectively Managed Public Relations Challenges

Examining how well-known brands have handled crises offers valuable lessons in reputation management and crisis communication. Here are three examples of food businesses that effectively managed public relations challenges and demonstrated strong crisis communication skills.

1. Tylenol's Response to the 1982 Poisoning Crisis

Although not a food brand, Tylenol's response to a poisoning crisis in 1982 is considered a gold standard in crisis management. After several people died from cyanide-laced Tylenol capsules, the company took immediate action to protect public safety and restore trust.

- Immediate Product Recall: Tylenol recalled 31 million bottles, prioritizing customer safety over profit. This unprecedented recall demonstrated Johnson & Johnson's commitment to consumer welfare.
- Transparent Communication: The company provided regular updates, engaged with the media, and kept the public informed of its safety measures.
- Impact: Tylenol's response led to industry-wide improvements in product packaging, including tamper-resistant seals, and restored the brand's reputation, proving that effective crisis management can rebuild trust.

2. KFC's "FCK" Campaign Following a Supply Chain Crisis

In 2018, KFC faced a major supply chain issue in the UK that led to a temporary shortage of chicken, forcing many locations to close. KFC's creative response turned a potential PR disaster into an opportunity to reinforce its brand personality.

- Humour and Transparency: KFC published a full-page apology ad in UK newspapers with the headline "FCK" (rearranging the letters in KFC), acknowledging the issue with humour and sincerity.

- Commitment to Resolution: The brand kept customers updated on efforts to resolve the crisis and reopen locations. This approach highlighted the brand's transparency and customer-centric focus.

- Impact: KFC's humorous, transparent response resonated with customers, turning a crisis into a brand-building opportunity that reinforced its image as a relatable, customer-focused business.

3. McDonald's Response to the "Hot Coffee" Lawsuit

In 1992, McDonald's faced a high-profile lawsuit after a customer suffered severe burns from spilled coffee. The incident attracted extensive media coverage and public scrutiny.

- Crisis Response and Communication: While initially hesitant to address the issue, McDonald's eventually implemented better labelling and cup designs to ensure customer safety. The brand communicated these changes to show commitment to improvement.

- Commitment to Customer Safety: McDonald's used the incident as an opportunity to update safety measures and re-evaluate its customer interaction protocols.

- Impact: Although initially challenging, McDonald's response to the coffee lawsuit ultimately led to improvements in industry-wide safety practices and demonstrated the importance of learning from crises.

Proactive and Transparent Crisis Management for Long-Term Success

Effective crisis management and reputation building

are essential for food businesses seeking to navigate challenges and maintain public trust. By preparing a crisis communication plan, responding to negative feedback with empathy, and prioritizing transparency and accountability, businesses can protect and even strengthen their brand reputation.

The examples of Tylenol, KFC, and McDonald's show that a well-handled crisis can reinforce a brand's commitment to customer safety and transparency. With the right strategies, food businesses can emerge from crises with a stronger, more trusted reputation, building long-term loyalty and resilience.

CHAPTER 20: DEVELOPING A LOYALTY PROGRAM AND RETENTION STRATEGIES

For any food business, cultivating a loyal customer base is key to long-term success. While attracting new customers is important, retaining existing customers often yields higher returns, as regular patrons are more likely to spend more, provide valuable feedback, and recommend the business to others. A well-designed loyalty program, coupled with effective retention strategies, encourages repeat business and strengthens customer relationships. This chapter will explore how to craft loyalty programs, techniques for turning occasional customers into regular patrons, and a case study of a successful loyalty program in the food industry.

Crafting Loyalty Programs to Encourage Repeat Business

Loyalty programs offer incentives that reward customers for their ongoing support, creating a mutually beneficial relationship between the business and its patrons. An effective loyalty program should be easy to understand, align with the brand, and provide real value to customers. Here are some essential elements for designing a successful loyalty program in the food industry.

1. Define Clear Objectives and Value Propositions

The first step in designing a loyalty program is defining its goals and value propositions. Understanding what the business aims to achieve—whether it's increasing visit frequency, boosting average spend, or encouraging social sharing—guides the program's structure and rewards.

- Identify Target Customers: Consider which segment of the customer base is most likely to engage with the loyalty program. For example, a café may target regular coffee drinkers, while a restaurant might focus on diners who frequent the establishment during lunch hours.

- Offer Valuable Rewards: Rewards should be meaningful and enticing to encourage participation. Common rewards include discounts, free items, or exclusive access to events. Offering tiered rewards can incentivize customers to reach higher spending levels.

- Example: Starbucks Rewards provides value by offering free beverages, food items, and personalized promotions. The program has tiered levels, with "Gold" members enjoying additional perks, encouraging customers to visit frequently to reach this status.

2. Choose the Right Program Type

There are several types of loyalty programs, each with unique benefits. Selecting the right program type depends on the business model, customer preferences, and desired engagement level.

- Point-Based Programs: Customers earn points for each purchase, which can be redeemed for rewards. This type of program is popular because it's straightforward and allows customers to track their progress.
- Visit-Based Programs: In a visit-based program, customers receive rewards based on the number of visits rather than the amount spent. This model is effective for fast-casual restaurants and cafés where increasing foot traffic is a priority.
- Subscription-Based Programs: Subscription-based loyalty programs involve a monthly or annual fee for exclusive benefits, such as discounts, free delivery, or members-only events. This type of program appeals to loyal customers who visit frequently.

- Example: Pret A Manger's "Coffee Subscription" allows customers to pay a monthly fee for unlimited coffee, encouraging regular visits and providing value to frequent customers.

3. Use Digital Platforms to Enhance Engagement

Digital loyalty platforms streamline program management, making it easy for customers to track their rewards, receive updates, and redeem points. Many food businesses use mobile apps or integrate loyalty programs with POS (point of sale) systems to enhance customer engagement.

- Mobile Apps: Mobile apps are convenient for

customers to track their rewards, receive personalized promotions, and manage their points. Push notifications can be used to remind customers of rewards and special offers.

- Integrated POS Systems: Integrating the loyalty program with the POS system simplifies tracking and redemption for both the customer and the business, providing a seamless experience.

- Example: Dunkin' uses its DD Perks app to engage customers with personalized offers, location-based rewards, and exclusive promotions. The app's ease of use and attractive incentives have contributed to high levels of customer engagement.

4. Incorporate Personalization and Exclusive Benefits

Personalized offers and exclusive benefits make customers feel valued and encourage loyalty. By leveraging customer data, food businesses can tailor rewards and promotions based on purchasing behaviour and preferences.

- Targeted Promotions: Offering discounts on favourite items or sending birthday rewards adds a personal touch that enhances the customer experience.

- Exclusive Access: Providing exclusive access to limited-time menu items, events, or special tastings creates excitement and adds value for loyalty program members.

- Example: Chick-fil-A's "Chick-fil-A One" rewards program uses data to personalize rewards based on each customer's order history. Members receive surprise rewards and birthday offers, making them feel appreciated and valued.

5. Create a Sense of Community and Engagement

A successful loyalty program fosters a sense of community, turning customers into brand advocates. Social media, events, and referral programs encourage customers to engage with the brand outside of regular visits and spread the word about their positive experiences.

- Social Media Engagement: Encourage loyalty members to share their rewards on social media, using hashtags or tagging the business. This not only increases brand visibility but also makes members feel part of a larger community.
- Referral Programs: Offering rewards for referrals incentivizes existing customers to bring in new patrons, expanding the customer base while rewarding loyal customers.
- Example: Sweetgreen's referral program offers rewards to both referrers and new customers, creating a win-win situation that increases customer acquisition while strengthening loyalty among current customers.

Techniques for Turning Occasional Customers into Regular Patrons

Turning occasional customers into regular patrons requires a blend of strategic incentives, personalized engagement, and exceptional service. Here are some techniques to encourage customers to visit more frequently and develop a lasting relationship with the brand.

1. Offer Time-Limited Promotions to Encourage Repeat Visits

Time-limited promotions create a sense of urgency, encouraging customers to return within a specific period. These can include discounts on the next visit, seasonal specials, or limited-time rewards.

- Bounce-Back Offers: Providing a discount or free item on the customer's next visit within a set timeframe (e.g., "Come back within 7 days for 10% off") encourages immediate repeat business.
- Seasonal or Holiday Promotions: Seasonal promotions, such as holiday-themed menu items or discounts, create excitement and give customers a reason to return regularly.
- Example: Krispy Kreme's limited-time seasonal donuts and promotions like "Talk Like a Pirate Day" generate buzz and encourage fans to visit to try the new flavours before they're gone.

2. Reward Consistency with Visit-Based Milestones

Rewarding customers based on visit frequency rather than spending amount incentivizes consistent visits and reinforces the habit of returning. Milestone rewards for every set number of visits (e.g., every 10th visit) make customers feel recognized for their loyalty.

- Milestone Rewards: Acknowledging customers for hitting milestones, such as "10th Visit Free," encourages them to return frequently.
- Punch Cards or Digital Check-Ins: Punch cards or digital check-in rewards are simple yet effective tools for

visit-based programs, particularly for smaller businesses looking to encourage regular traffic.

- Example: Many independent coffee shops offer digital or physical punch cards that reward customers with a free drink after every 10 purchases, encouraging regular visits and rewarding loyalty.

3. Use Data to Personalize the Experience

Collecting data on customer preferences allows businesses to personalize interactions, offering tailored recommendations or customized promotions. Personalized experiences make customers feel valued and more likely to return.

- Customized Offers: By tracking customer purchases, businesses can offer discounts on frequently ordered items or send alerts for favourite seasonal items.
- Targeted Marketing Campaigns: Email or SMS marketing campaigns that cater to individual preferences, such as vegetarian-friendly promotions, resonate more with customers and encourage repeat visits.

- Example: Panera Bread's "MyPanera" program uses customer data to send personalized offers, such as discounts on frequently purchased items or exclusive previews of new menu items, fostering loyalty and repeat visits.

4. Provide an Exceptional Customer Experience Every Time

While promotions and loyalty rewards are powerful, the most important factor in converting occasional customers to regulars is delivering exceptional service consistently. Positive interactions, quick service, and friendly staff create memorable experiences that inspire loyalty.

- Train Staff for Consistency: Ensuring that all staff members are trained to provide friendly, efficient service contributes to a consistently positive experience.
- Solicit and Act on Feedback: Gathering customer feedback and making improvements shows customers that their opinions are valued, reinforcing their decision to return.
- Example: In-N-Out Burger's focus on consistent quality, friendly service, and a clean environment has contributed to its loyal customer base, as patrons know they can expect a reliable experience at every location.

5. Build a Sense of Belonging and Community

Creating a welcoming environment where customers feel a sense of belonging encourages them to return. Engaging customers through events, social media, and loyalty program perks fosters a connection to the brand.

- Community Events and Engagement: Hosting community events, such as tastings or workshops, invites customers to interact with the brand on a more personal level.
- Social Media Interaction: Actively engaging with customers on social media—whether by reposting user-generated content, responding to comments, or highlighting loyalty members—creates a sense of community.
- Example: Shake Shack's "Shack Fan Club" encourages

members to share their experiences and offers exclusive merchandise, creating a community atmosphere that resonates with loyal customers.

Case Study: Starbucks Rewards Program

Starbucks Rewards is one of the most successful loyalty programs in the food industry, transforming occasional coffee drinkers into dedicated patrons through a mix of rewards, personalization, and convenience. Here's how the Starbucks Rewards program has driven customer loyalty and become a model for successful loyalty programs.

1. Program Structure and Incentives

Starbucks Rewards operates on a point-based system where customers earn "Stars" for each purchase. Stars can be redeemed for free drinks, food items, and exclusive rewards. The program has a tiered structure with "Green" and "Gold" levels, with Gold members receiving extra perks, such as monthly double Star days and access to special items.

2. Convenience and Digital Integration

The Starbucks Rewards program is fully integrated into the Starbucks app, allowing customers to track their Stars, receive offers, and make mobile orders. This seamless integration makes it easy for customers to manage their rewards and order ahead, providing a streamlined experience.

3. Personalization and Exclusive Benefits

Starbucks uses data from the Rewards program to

send personalized offers, such as discounts on frequently purchased items or birthday rewards. Gold members also receive access to exclusive menu items, special offers, and early access to seasonal drinks.

4. Community Engagement and Social Media

Starbucks actively engages with its loyal customer base on social media, where it shares updates about new products, features user-generated content, and promotes loyalty program benefits. This engagement fosters a sense of community among members and keeps them informed and excited about new rewards.

- Impact: Starbucks Rewards has driven significant growth for the brand, with millions of members participating worldwide. The program's mix of convenience, personalization, and exclusive benefits has made it a model for successful loyalty programs in the food industry.

Building Customer Loyalty and Retention for Long-Term Success

Developing a loyalty program and implementing retention strategies are essential steps for food businesses looking to build strong, lasting customer relationships. A well-crafted loyalty program, combined with personalized engagement, community building, and consistent service, encourages customers to return and fosters a loyal customer base.

As illustrated by Starbucks Rewards, a successful loyalty program aligns with customer values, offers meaningful rewards, and creates a sense of community. By adopting similar strategies, food businesses can turn occasional customers into devoted patrons, driving growth and establishing a foundation for long-term success.

CHAPTER 21: SCALING YOUR FOOD BUSINESS

Scaling a food business involves expanding its reach, either by opening new locations, franchising, or diversifying with new product lines. Each option presents unique financial and operational challenges, but with a strategic approach, food businesses can grow sustainably and tap into new markets. This chapter explores expansion strategies, discusses the challenges associated with scaling, and highlights examples of successful food brands that expanded effectively.

Options for Expansion: Opening New Locations, Franchising, or Product Lines

Scaling a food business is a major step that requires careful consideration of resources, brand alignment, and market potential. Here are three primary expansion options for food entrepreneurs.

1. Opening New Locations

One of the most common ways to scale a food business is by opening additional locations. Expanding geographically allows a business to reach new customer bases while maintaining full control over operations, quality, and brand identity.

- Single vs. Multiple Locations: Starting with a single additional location is often the best approach for refining expansion strategies before moving to multiple outlets. Each new location should be evaluated for demographics, market demand, and proximity to competitors.

- Consistency and Quality Control: As the business scales, ensuring consistency in quality, service, and customer experience across locations becomes essential. Standardizing processes, training staff, and maintaining strong management practices support brand consistency.

- Example: In-N-Out Burger has expanded gradually, focusing on high standards of quality and a carefully controlled supply chain. This approach has helped maintain the brand's reputation and loyal customer base as it expands.

2. Franchising

Franchising allows food businesses to grow rapidly by partnering with franchisees who operate additional locations. This model requires a robust support system and training program to ensure that franchisees can replicate the brand's success while maintaining consistency.

- Franchise Model Requirements: Developing a franchise model involves creating a comprehensive franchise agreement, establishing training and operational guidelines, and implementing systems for quality control. Franchisees must be supported with ongoing guidance to maintain brand standards.

- Benefits and Risks: Franchising offers the advantage of scaling with less capital investment from the original owner, as franchisees contribute funds for expansion. However, franchisees must adhere to the brand's standards, as inconsistent service or quality can harm the brand's reputation.

- Example: Subway used franchising to scale quickly, becoming one of the world's largest restaurant chains. By providing extensive support to franchisees and standardizing processes, Subway achieved rapid expansion across international markets.

3. Product Line Expansion

Expanding into new product lines—such as bottled sauces, pre-packaged meals, or branded merchandise—allows businesses to reach customers beyond their physical locations. This approach can help diversify revenue streams and build brand visibility.

- Retail and E-commerce: Selling products through retail stores or e-commerce platforms allows customers to engage with the brand from home. A strong online presence and partnerships with retailers can drive product line success.

- Aligning with Brand Identity: New product lines should align with the brand's core identity and values. A restaurant known for artisanal sauces might launch a line of bottled sauces, while a bakery could sell packaged pastries or baking kits.

- Example: Magnolia Bakery successfully expanded by selling its famous banana pudding and other desserts in grocery stores and online. This product line extension allowed the brand to reach a wider audience beyond its brick-and-mortar locations.

Financial and Operational Challenges of Scaling

While scaling offers opportunities for growth, it also presents financial and operational challenges. Managing these challenges effectively requires careful planning, resource allocation, and risk assessment.

1. Capital Requirements and Funding Options

Scaling a food business demands significant financial investment for new locations, equipment, inventory, and staffing. Entrepreneurs must assess funding options to secure the necessary capital without compromising cash flow.

- Self-Funding and Savings: Some businesses use existing profits or savings to fund expansion. This approach offers full control but may limit the pace of growth.
- Small Business Loans: Small business loans or lines of credit provide capital for expansion with manageable repayment terms. Many food businesses rely on loans to cover initial costs for new locations.
- Investors and Venture Capital: Securing investment from venture capitalists or angel investors provides capital in exchange for equity. While this option accelerates growth, it also requires business owners to relinquish some control.

- Example: Shake Shack initially used investment funding to expand its locations and build a brand presence beyond New York City. The brand's careful expansion strategy helped it attract additional investors and eventually led to a successful IPO.

2. Maintaining Quality and Consistency

As businesses scale, maintaining consistent quality across multiple locations or product lines becomes challenging. Customers expect the same quality and experience wherever they engage with the brand.

- Standardized Operating Procedures (SOPs): Developing SOPs for food preparation, service, and cleanliness helps ensure that each location meets the same standards. Documenting these procedures allows for easier training and accountability.
- Rigorous Staff Training: A strong training program ensures that employees understand the brand's values, recipes, and service expectations. Regular training sessions, both on-site and online, reinforce these standards.
- Centralized Supply Chain Management: Establishing centralized purchasing and supplier relationships ensures consistency in ingredients, packaging, and pricing. Many food brands rely on a centralized distribution system to support multiple locations.

- Example: Chipotle's commitment to "Food with Integrity" has driven its supply chain decisions, ensuring that each location sources high-quality, ethically sourced ingredients. This consistency strengthens the brand's reputation and customer trust.

3. Operational Complexity and Management Challenges

Scaling a food business increases operational complexity, requiring more oversight, management, and coordination across locations or product lines. Efficient management structures and systems are essential for maintaining operational efficiency.

- Delegating Management Roles: Hiring experienced managers for each location allows business owners to focus on strategic growth while ensuring day-to-day operations run smoothly. Creating a regional management structure can improve oversight.

- Implementing Technology Solutions: POS systems, inventory tracking software, and employee scheduling tools streamline operations and help manage multiple locations effectively.

- Quality Assurance Audits: Conducting regular audits for quality assurance across locations or product lines ensures that standards are consistently met, identifying and addressing issues before they impact the brand's reputation.

- Example: Starbucks uses sophisticated technology and standardized processes to manage thousands of locations worldwide. Its emphasis on employee training and efficient technology has allowed Starbucks to maintain consistent quality across all markets.

4. Adapting to Market Demands and Local Preferences

Expanding into new markets requires flexibility to adapt to local preferences while staying true to the brand's identity. Market research helps identify customer preferences, competitive landscapes, and pricing expectations in different regions.

- Customizing Menus for Regional Appeal: Some brands offer region-specific menu items to appeal to local tastes. For example, a fast-casual chain might introduce vegetarian options in a location with high demand for plant-based foods.

- Pricing Adjustments for New Markets: Pricing strategies may need to be adjusted to align with regional economic conditions, cost of living, and customer expectations.

- Example: McDonald's adapts its menu in different countries, offering items that reflect local flavours and dietary preferences. This flexibility has helped McDonald's build a global presence while staying relevant in diverse markets.

Examples of Brands that Successfully Scaled Their Operations

Several food brands have successfully scaled their operations by leveraging strategic growth approaches, from opening new locations to launching product lines. Here are three examples that showcase effective scaling strategies.

1. Shake Shack: Gradual and Quality-Focused Expansion

Shake Shack began as a hot dog stand in New York City and has since grown into an internationally recognized fast-casual chain. The brand's commitment to quality and gradual expansion strategy has been key to its success.

- Controlled Expansion: Rather than expanding aggressively, Shake Shack opted for a gradual approach, opening select locations in high-demand areas. This allowed the brand to maintain quality and control costs while building a loyal following.

- Focus on Consistency and Quality: Shake Shack prioritized quality in both food and service, ensuring that each new location met the brand's high standards. This focus on consistency has built customer trust and enhanced brand reputation.

- Outcome: Shake Shack's strategic, quality-focused growth has helped it achieve international recognition, with loyal customers who appreciate the brand's commitment to premium ingredients and unique dining experience.

2. Panera Bread: Scaling Through Acquisitions and Centralized Operations

Panera Bread expanded from a regional bakery-café to a nationwide chain by acquiring existing bakery brands and implementing centralized operations. This approach enabled rapid growth without compromising quality.

- Acquisitions and Rebranding: Panera's acquisition of bakery chains in various regions allowed it to enter new markets with an established customer base. Rebranding these locations under the Panera name created consistency across the chain.

- Centralized Production Facilities: Panera established centralized production facilities to prepare dough and ingredients for its stores, ensuring consistent quality across locations while reducing operational costs.

- Outcome: Panera's acquisition strategy and centralized production have contributed to its growth into one of the largest fast-casual bakery chains in the U.S., with a reputation for quality and customer satisfaction.

3. Magnolia Bakery: Product Line Expansion and E-commerce Growth

Magnolia Bakery, known for its cupcakes and classic American desserts, scaled its brand by expanding its product lines and leveraging e-commerce to reach customers nationwide.

- Product Line Extensions: Magnolia introduced packaged versions of its popular desserts, including banana pudding and cupcakes, for retail sale. This product line expansion allowed the brand to reach a broader audience.
- E-commerce and Nationwide Shipping: By offering nationwide shipping, Magnolia Bakery enabled customers to order its products online, making it accessible to fans who couldn't visit a physical location.

- Outcome: Magnolia Bakery's strategic use of product line expansion and e-commerce has driven brand growth, allowing it to scale beyond its physical locations and create a strong national presence.

Strategic Scaling for Sustainable Growth

Scaling a food business is a complex but rewarding endeavour that requires a strategic approach to maintain quality, consistency, and customer satisfaction.

By choosing the right expansion model—whether through new locations, franchising, or product line extensions—food businesses can grow sustainably while strengthening brand identity.

The examples of Shake Shack, Panera Bread, and Magnolia Bakery illustrate that successful scaling depends on thoughtful planning, quality control, and adaptability. By addressing financial, operational, and market challenges head-on, food entrepreneurs can build a scalable brand that resonates with customers and drives long-term success.

CHAPTER 22: INTEGRATING SUSTAINABLE PRACTICES

In today's eco-conscious world, integrating sustainable practices has become essential for food businesses that want to attract environmentally aware consumers and contribute positively to the planet. Sustainability not only benefits the environment but also strengthens brand loyalty, improves operational efficiency, and aligns with shifting customer expectations. From sourcing responsibly to reducing waste, there are various ways food businesses can implement eco-friendly practices. This chapter explores the benefits of sustainability, methods for incorporating sustainable practices in sourcing, packaging, and waste management, and highlights a case study of a food business that has successfully embraced sustainability.

Benefits of Sustainability for Food Businesses and the

Environment

Adopting sustainable practices offers numerous benefits, both for food businesses and the environment. Businesses that prioritize sustainability gain a competitive edge by resonating with eco-conscious customers and building a positive brand image, while simultaneously reducing their ecological impact.

1. Enhancing Brand Image and Customer Loyalty

Consumers today are more likely to support businesses that demonstrate a commitment to sustainability. A food business that actively reduces waste, sources responsibly, and minimizes its environmental footprint can attract loyal customers who value ethical practices.

- Competitive Advantage: Sustainable practices set businesses apart from competitors by appealing to a growing demographic of eco-conscious customers.

- Customer Trust and Loyalty: Transparency in sustainability efforts, such as sharing the origins of ingredients or environmental initiatives, helps build trust and a loyal customer base.

- Example: Sweetgreen, a popular fast-casual salad chain, has built a reputation for using fresh, locally sourced ingredients and eco-friendly packaging, attracting a loyal following among health-conscious and environmentally aware consumers.

2. Reducing Operational Costs

Sustainable practices, such as energy-efficient equipment and waste reduction strategies, can result in cost savings over time. By using fewer resources and reducing waste, food businesses can decrease expenses and improve their bottom line.

  - Lower Utility Costs: Energy-efficient appliances and lighting reduce electricity bills, while water-saving fixtures lower water costs.
  - Minimizing Food Waste: Reducing food waste helps control inventory costs and lowers disposal expenses, allowing businesses to use ingredients more efficiently.

  - Example: Panera Bread has implemented energy-efficient equipment in its kitchens, helping reduce energy costs across its locations. This approach has led to savings that support the brand's commitment to sustainability.

3. Supporting Environmental Health and Conservation

   Sustainable practices have a direct positive impact on the environment, from conserving natural resources to reducing pollution. Sourcing responsibly and reducing waste support biodiversity, protect ecosystems, and contribute to a healthier planet.

  - Conserving Resources: By sourcing ingredients locally, businesses reduce carbon emissions associated with long-distance transportation. Reducing plastic packaging and switching to compostable materials further reduce the environmental burden.
  - Minimizing Pollution: Cutting down on waste, particularly non-recyclable or non-biodegradable materials, decreases the amount of waste in landfills and minimizes pollution.

  - Example: Starbucks has committed to reducing plastic waste by introducing reusable cups and phasing out single-use plastic straws. This initiative reduces plastic waste and promotes more sustainable options for customers.

Implementing Eco-Friendly Practices in Sourcing, Packaging, and Waste Management

Food businesses can integrate sustainability into various aspects of their operations, from sourcing ingredients responsibly to managing waste effectively. Each step in the supply chain presents opportunities for eco-friendly practices that enhance sustainability.

1. Eco-Friendly Sourcing

Sourcing ingredients sustainably involves selecting suppliers who prioritize environmental stewardship and ethical practices. Sustainable sourcing practices ensure that ingredients are produced in ways that protect natural resources, respect workers' rights, and support local economies.

- Local Sourcing: Buying from local farmers and producers reduces carbon emissions from transportation and supports the local economy. Additionally, locally sourced ingredients are often fresher and require less packaging.
- Seasonal Ingredients: Using seasonal ingredients reduces the need for imported produce, which often requires significant resources for transportation and storage. Seasonal menus also showcase the natural flavours of ingredients at their peak.
- Organic and Fair-Trade Ingredients: Organic and fair-trade certifications ensure that ingredients are grown without harmful chemicals and that workers receive

fair wages, supporting environmental health and social responsibility.

- Example: The farm-to-table restaurant Chez Panisse sources ingredients from local farms and focuses on organic, seasonal produce. This approach minimizes environmental impact while supporting sustainable agriculture.

2. Sustainable Packaging

Packaging is a significant source of waste in the food industry, and switching to sustainable packaging materials can reduce a business's environmental footprint. Eco-friendly packaging options, such as compostable materials and recyclable containers, help minimize waste.

- Biodegradable and Compostable Packaging: Biodegradable and compostable packaging materials break down naturally, reducing waste in landfills. Many food businesses use compostable containers, utensils, and straws to reduce single-use plastic.
- Recyclable and Reusable Options: Recyclable materials, such as glass, cardboard, and certain plastics, can be reused, reducing waste. Offering reusable containers or incentives for customers who bring their own can further support sustainability.
- Minimalistic Packaging: Using minimal packaging reduces the amount of material waste. Businesses can consider reducing or eliminating packaging for items where it's not necessary.

- Example: Chipotle uses compostable bowls, napkins made from recycled materials, and limited packaging to reduce its environmental impact. The company's packaging choices reflect its commitment to sustainability.

3. Waste Management and Reduction

Effective waste management is essential for sustainability in the food industry. Reducing food waste, recycling, and composting help divert waste from landfills and support resource conservation.

- Food Waste Reduction: Businesses can reduce food waste by accurately tracking inventory, repurposing surplus ingredients, and donating excess food to local charities. Efficient portion control and creative menu planning also help minimize waste.
- Composting: Composting food scraps and biodegradable waste reduces the amount of waste sent to landfills. Many restaurants partner with composting services to handle organic waste responsibly.
- Recycling Programs: Implementing a recycling program for paper, cardboard, glass, and plastic waste supports sustainable practices. Proper labelling and staff training can improve recycling rates.
- Example: Blue Hill at Stone Barns, a farm-to-table restaurant in New York, has adopted a "waste not" approach, repurposing food scraps into creative dishes and composting organic waste. This commitment to zero waste supports sustainable dining practices.

4. Energy and Water Conservation

Reducing energy and water consumption is another important aspect of sustainability. Efficient use of resources lowers operating costs and minimizes the environmental impact of food businesses.

- Energy-Efficient Appliances: Investing in energy-efficient kitchen appliances, such as convection ovens and LED lighting, reduces electricity consumption and lowers utility bills.
- Water-Saving Fixtures: Installing low-flow faucets and dishwashers helps conserve water, a critical resource in many areas. Efficient water use also reduces utility expenses.
- Smart Thermostats and Lighting Controls: Automated thermostats and motion-activated lighting systems help reduce energy waste, particularly during off-peak hours.

- Example: McDonald's has implemented energy-saving equipment and water-efficient appliances in its restaurants globally, reducing its environmental impact and supporting its commitment to sustainability.

Case Study: Sweetgreen's Commitment to Sustainability

Sweetgreen, a fast-casual salad chain, has become a leader in sustainability within the food industry. The brand's commitment to eco-friendly practices, from ingredient sourcing to packaging, has helped Sweetgreen build a loyal customer base that values sustainability.

1. Locally Sourced Ingredients

Sweetgreen prioritizes locally sourced ingredients, partnering with regional farmers and suppliers to obtain fresh, seasonal produce. This approach reduces transportation emissions, supports local agriculture, and ensures that customers enjoy high-quality, fresh ingredients.

- Seasonal Menu: Sweetgreen's menu changes seasonally to reflect the availability of local produce. This focus on seasonal ingredients reduces reliance on imported goods and showcases fresh, regional flavours.

- Transparency in Sourcing: Sweetgreen highlights its farm partners on its website and in-store displays, allowing customers to see exactly where their food comes from. This transparency builds trust and reinforces the brand's commitment to sustainability.

2. Sustainable Packaging

Sweetgreen has made significant strides in reducing its reliance on single-use plastics by using compostable and recyclable packaging. The company's bowls, lids, and utensils are made from compostable materials, helping to minimize waste.

- Compostable Bowls and Utensils: Sweetgreen's use of compostable bowls and utensils aligns with its sustainability goals and appeals to environmentally conscious customers. The brand encourages customers to compost their packaging whenever possible.

- Reusable Options: Sweetgreen also offers reusable bowls for customers, providing a discount to those who bring their own. This initiative helps reduce single-use waste and promotes eco-friendly habits among customers.

3. Waste Reduction and Food Donation

Sweetgreen is committed to reducing food waste through accurate forecasting and efficient inventory management. Any surplus ingredients are donated to local food banks, ensuring that unused food benefits the community rather than going to waste.

- Inventory Management: By closely monitoring ingredient levels, Sweetgreen reduces excess stock and minimizes food spoilage. This efficient management approach supports waste reduction while controlling costs.

- Food Donations: Sweetgreen partners with local organizations to donate any surplus food, contributing to community welfare and supporting food security.

4. Energy and Water Conservation

Sweetgreen's sustainability efforts also extend to energy and water conservation. The brand uses energy-efficient appliances and promotes water-saving practices in its kitchens.

- Efficient Appliances: By using energy-efficient kitchen equipment and LED lighting, Sweetgreen reduces its energy consumption, which helps lower its carbon footprint and operating costs.

- Conservation Practices: Sweetgreen educates its staff on water-saving practices, such as using low-flow faucets and minimizing water waste during food prep.

- Outcome: Sweetgreen's comprehensive approach to sustainability has helped the brand attract a loyal customer base, strengthen its eco-friendly reputation, and reduce its environmental impact. Its commitment to transparency, sustainable sourcing, and waste reduction has made Sweetgreen a model for other food businesses looking to adopt eco-friendly practices.

Building a Sustainable Future for Food Businesses

Integrating sustainable practices is not only beneficial for the environment but also strengthens brand identity, enhances customer loyalty, and contributes to operational efficiency. By implementing eco-friendly practices in sourcing, packaging, waste management, and resource conservation, food businesses can reduce their environmental impact and appeal to a growing market of eco-conscious consumers.

As demonstrated by Sweetgreen, a commitment to sustainability goes beyond individual practices; it requires a holistic approach that aligns with the brand's values and resonates with customers. By adopting similar strategies, food entrepreneurs can create a positive impact on the planet while building a successful, future-ready brand.

CHAPTER 23: TECHNOLOGY AND INNOVATION IN FOOD ENTREPRENEURSHIP

Technology has transformed the food industry, revolutionizing how businesses operate, engage with customers, and expand their reach. From advanced point-of-sale (POS) systems to food delivery apps and data analytics, technology offers food entrepreneurs new ways to streamline operations, improve efficiency, and enhance the customer experience. In this chapter, we explore current technology trends, discuss how technology can drive operational efficiency and customer engagement, and provide case studies of food businesses that have successfully embraced technological innovation.

Trends in Technology: From POS Systems to Food Delivery Apps

The rapid evolution of technology has introduced several key innovations that have redefined the food industry. These tools not only make operations smoother but also help businesses stay competitive in a fast-paced market.

1. Point-of-Sale (POS) Systems

Modern POS systems go beyond traditional cash registers, offering an array of features to streamline operations, track sales, and enhance the customer experience. Advanced POS systems integrate with inventory management, customer loyalty programs, and financial reporting.

- Integrated Inventory Tracking: POS systems that sync with inventory allow businesses to monitor stock levels in real-time, reducing waste and preventing stockouts.
- Mobile POS: Mobile POS solutions enable staff to process orders and payments directly at the table, speeding up service and enhancing the customer experience.
- Sales Analytics: POS systems generate detailed sales reports, providing insights into peak hours, top-selling items, and seasonal trends, helping businesses make data-driven decisions.
- Example: Toast, a popular POS system for restaurants, offers mobile ordering, inventory management, and sales analytics. Many restaurants use Toast to optimize their operations and enhance customer service.

2. Food Delivery Apps and Online Ordering

The demand for food delivery has surged, driven by the convenience of ordering through apps. Food delivery apps like UberEats, DoorDash, and Grubhub allow restaurants to reach a broader customer base, providing opportunities for growth without requiring additional physical space.

- Third-Party Delivery Platforms: These platforms connect restaurants with a vast customer network, expanding reach without the need to invest in delivery infrastructure.
- Branded Online Ordering: Many businesses offer online ordering through their own websites or apps, allowing for direct engagement with customers and eliminating third-party fees.
- Subscription and Membership Models: Some businesses use subscription services, allowing customers to receive regular deliveries, such as weekly meal kits or coffee orders.

- Example: Chipotle has developed its own digital ordering platform, allowing customers to place orders through the Chipotle app and website, with options for pickup or delivery. This digital strategy has increased convenience for customers and boosted sales.

3. Self-Service Kiosks and Contactless Ordering

Self-service kiosks and contactless ordering have gained popularity, particularly in fast-casual and quick-service restaurants. These solutions reduce wait times, minimize contact, and allow customers to customize their orders, improving the overall dining experience.

- Self-Service Kiosks: Customers place orders and make payments at kiosks, reducing lines and allowing staff to focus on other tasks. Kiosks also provide visual displays for customization options, which can increase average order sizes.

- Contactless Ordering and Payments: QR codes and NFC (near-field communication) technology enable customers to order and pay directly from their smartphones, reducing physical touchpoints.

- Example: McDonald's has implemented self-service kiosks in many locations, allowing customers to customize orders and pay without waiting in line. The kiosks have streamlined ordering, improved order accuracy, and reduced pressure on counter staff.

4. Data Analytics and Customer Insights

Data analytics help food businesses understand customer preferences, identify trends, and make informed decisions. By collecting data on sales, customer demographics, and feedback, businesses can create targeted marketing campaigns, optimize menus, and improve customer satisfaction.

- Customer Behaviour Tracking: Analytics tools track how often customers visit, what items they order, and average spend. This data can inform marketing strategies and loyalty programs.

- Predictive Analytics: By analysing historical data, businesses can forecast demand, optimize staffing, and adjust inventory based on projected sales trends.

- Personalized Marketing: Data-driven insights allow businesses to personalize promotions, loyalty rewards, and recommendations based on customer behaviour.

- Example: Starbucks uses data analytics through its mobile app to offer personalized promotions, track customer preferences, and adjust inventory based on purchasing patterns. This tailored approach has helped Starbucks improve customer engagement and boost sales.

5. Automation in the Kitchen

Automation is increasingly used in kitchens to improve efficiency and consistency. Automated equipment, from robotic food prep stations to automated fryers, can reduce labour costs, enhance precision, and improve the speed of service.

- Robotic Food Prep: Some fast-casual restaurants use robots to automate repetitive tasks, such as chopping, mixing, or frying, reducing labour needs and ensuring consistent quality.
- Automated Beverage Systems: Automated beverage dispensers reduce wait times for customers and improve order accuracy, especially in high-volume locations.
- Order Management Screens: Digital screens that display incoming orders streamline communication between the front-of-house and kitchen staff, reducing errors and speeding up preparation times.

- Example: Creator, a San Francisco-based restaurant, uses a burger-making robot to prepare gourmet burgers with minimal human intervention. The robot's precision and speed enhance quality control and reduce wait times.

Using Technology to Streamline Operations and Reach

Customers

Technology enables food businesses to improve efficiency, reduce costs, and enhance customer experience in various ways. By leveraging digital tools, businesses can better manage inventory, refine customer engagement, and streamline operations.

1. Enhancing Efficiency and Reducing Waste

Technology solutions like inventory management software and automated ordering systems minimize waste by optimizing stock levels, improving accuracy, and reducing over-ordering. Efficient inventory management is essential for cost control and reducing food waste.

- Real-Time Inventory Tracking: Real-time inventory tracking helps businesses monitor stock levels, track expiration dates, and receive alerts for low stock items, minimizing spoilage and waste.
- Automated Reordering: Inventory systems that automatically reorder ingredients based on pre-set thresholds help maintain optimal stock levels and reduce the risk of running out of key ingredients.
- Example: Panera Bread uses a digital inventory management system to track ingredient levels, optimize ordering, and reduce waste. This efficient approach supports its commitment to sustainability and reduces operating costs.

2. Improving the Customer Experience with Digital Tools

Digital tools enhance the customer experience by offering convenient options for ordering, customizing meals, and managing loyalty rewards. By providing seamless, technology-driven interactions, businesses can attract and retain customers more effectively.

- Loyalty Programs: Digital loyalty programs allow customers to track rewards, redeem points, and receive personalized offers through mobile apps. This enhances customer retention and encourages repeat visits.

- Order Customization: Self-service kiosks and apps with customization options allow customers to tailor their orders, improving satisfaction and increasing average order value.

- Example: Chick-fil-A's app offers a digital loyalty program that tracks points, sends personalized promotions, and allows for mobile ordering. The app's ease of use and attractive rewards have contributed to high customer engagement.

3. Expanding Reach Through Digital Marketing and Social Media

Social media, digital marketing, and online ordering platforms allow food businesses to reach a broader audience, attract new customers, and engage with loyal patrons. Digital marketing tools, such as email campaigns and social media ads, drive awareness and build a brand presence.

- Social Media Engagement: Platforms like Instagram, Facebook, and TikTok help businesses showcase their offerings, engage with followers, and share updates. Posting regularly on social media increases visibility and builds a loyal online community.

- Targeted Advertising: Digital advertising allows

businesses to reach specific demographics based on location, interests, and browsing behaviour. This targeted approach maximizes marketing budgets and attracts relevant customers.

- Email Marketing Campaigns: Email marketing campaigns keep customers informed of new menu items, special offers, and events. Many food businesses use email lists to communicate with loyalty program members and promote limited-time deals.

- Example: Taco Bell uses social media creatively to engage with customers, launching interactive campaigns, promoting new menu items, and connecting with fans in real-time. This approach has strengthened Taco Bell's brand presence and expanded its reach among younger audiences.

4. Ensuring Consistency Across Locations with Standardized Systems

For multi-location food businesses, consistency in service, quality, and customer experience is critical. Standardized systems, from POS and inventory management to employee training, help ensure that all locations operate under the same standards.

- Centralized Inventory and Ordering Systems: Centralized systems allow managers to monitor inventory levels, order supplies, and track sales data across multiple locations, improving consistency and operational control.

- Training Programs and Digital Manuals: Online training platforms and digital employee manuals ensure that staff members receive consistent training on procedures, recipes, and customer service practices.

- Digital Quality Assurance: Some businesses use technology to conduct quality checks, record inspections, and generate compliance reports, ensuring that all locations meet brand standards.

 - Example: Chipotle uses a centralized POS system and digital training modules to ensure consistency across its locations. The system allows Chipotle to monitor performance metrics, inventory, and employee training, maintaining high standards chain-wide.

Case Studies on Technology Adoption in the Food Industry

The following case studies showcase how food businesses have effectively adopted technology to drive growth, enhance customer experiences, and improve operational efficiency.

1. Domino's: Embracing Digital Ordering and Delivery Innovation

Domino's has become a leader in digital innovation, transforming its business with a focus on online ordering, delivery tracking, and technology-driven convenience.

 - Order Tracking and Delivery Innovation: Domino's "Domino's Tracker" allows customers to follow their order from preparation to delivery in real-time, providing transparency and improving customer satisfaction.
 - Multi-Platform Ordering: Domino's offers ordering through its website, app, smart speakers, and even social media channels, providing maximum convenience for

customers.

- Investment in AI and Machine Learning: Domino's uses machine learning to predict demand, optimize delivery routes, and improve order accuracy. This investment in AI supports efficient operations and reduces delivery times.

- Outcome: Domino's digital transformation has resulted in increased customer loyalty, faster delivery, and significant revenue growth. Its emphasis on convenience and innovation has strengthened its market position.

2. Panera Bread: Enhancing Customer Experience Through Digital Technology

Panera Bread has invested heavily in digital technology, enhancing both the customer experience and operational efficiency. Its innovations include self-service kiosks, digital ordering, and rapid-pickup options.

- Rapid Pick-Up and Online Ordering: Customers can place orders online or through the Panera app, choosing a specific pick-up time to avoid waiting in line. This feature has become popular among busy customers who value convenience.

- Kiosk Ordering and Customization: Self-service kiosks allow customers to customize their orders, view nutritional information, and pay directly, reducing wait times and improving order accuracy.

- Loyalty Integration: Panera's "MyPanera" loyalty program is integrated into the app, allowing customers to earn and redeem rewards seamlessly while tracking their favourite menu items.

- Outcome: Panera's commitment to digital innovation has boosted customer satisfaction and loyalty, with digital sales accounting for a significant portion of the brand's total revenue.

3. Sweetgreen: Using Data and Technology for Efficiency and Sustainability

Sweetgreen, a fast-casual salad chain, uses technology to improve operational efficiency, track inventory, and provide a seamless customer experience. The brand's digital-first approach has allowed it to scale effectively and maintain high standards of sustainability.

- Mobile Ordering and App Integration: Sweetgreen's app enables customers to order ahead, customize salads, and receive updates on seasonal menu items. The app's ease of use has driven customer engagement.
- Data-Driven Inventory Management: Sweetgreen uses data analytics to monitor ingredient usage and optimize stock levels, minimizing waste and supporting sustainable practices.
- Transparent Sourcing and Impact Tracking: The app also provides transparency on ingredient sourcing and sustainability initiatives, appealing to eco-conscious customers.
- Outcome: Sweetgreen's tech-driven approach has supported its growth, enabling the brand to maintain efficiency and sustainability as it scales.

Embracing Technology for Growth and Innovation

Integrating technology into food businesses allows

entrepreneurs to streamline operations, enhance customer experience, and drive growth in a competitive market. From POS systems and delivery apps to data analytics and kitchen automation, technology offers tools that improve efficiency and customer satisfaction.

The examples of Domino's, Panera Bread, and Sweetgreen highlight how adopting digital solutions can transform a food business, making it more responsive, scalable, and customer-focused. By staying ahead of tech trends and embracing innovation, food entrepreneurs can build resilient brands that thrive in today's digital landscape.

CHAPTER 24: PREPARING FOR THE FUTURE OF FOOD ENTREPRENEURSHIP

The food industry is constantly evolving, driven by shifts in consumer behaviour, technological advancements, and global trends. For food entrepreneurs, staying attuned to emerging trends and preparing for future market shifts is essential to build resilient, adaptable businesses that thrive over the long term. This chapter explores emerging trends in the food industry—such as plant-based foods, personalized nutrition, and culinary tourism—outlines strategic planning approaches for future market shifts, and provides insights into cultivating a forward-thinking, resilient mindset.

Emerging Trends in the Food Industry

The food industry is shaped by shifting consumer preferences, advancements in food science, and a growing focus on sustainability and health. Staying ahead of these trends allows food businesses to remain relevant, attract new customers, and establish themselves as leaders in innovation.

1. Plant-Based Foods and Alternative Proteins

The demand for plant-based foods and alternative proteins has surged, fuelled by health-conscious consumers and environmental concerns. Plant-based diets are moving beyond niche markets to become mainstream, and innovative products like meat substitutes, dairy alternatives, and plant-based snacks are widely popular.

- Consumer Health and Wellness: Many consumers are choosing plant-based foods for health reasons, seeking lower cholesterol, reduced inflammation, and improved heart health.
- Environmental Impact: Plant-based diets have a lower environmental footprint, using fewer resources and generating fewer greenhouse gas emissions than animal-based foods.
- Product Innovation: Innovations in food science have led to the development of alternative proteins, such as lab-grown meat, pea protein, and algae-based foods, which closely mimic the taste and texture of traditional animal products.
- Example: Beyond Meat and Impossible Foods are

pioneering brands in the alternative protein market. Both companies have developed plant-based burgers that replicate the taste and texture of meat, appealing to consumers who are reducing or eliminating animal products from their diets.

2. Personalized Nutrition and Functional Foods

As technology and nutrition science advance, consumers increasingly seek food options tailored to their individual health needs. Personalized nutrition and functional foods that offer specific health benefits are gaining traction, with consumers turning to food as a tool for wellness and disease prevention.

- Dietary Customization: With access to tools like DNA testing and wearable health devices, consumers are becoming more aware of their unique dietary needs. Personalized nutrition plans address specific health goals, such as weight management, improved gut health, and enhanced energy.

- Functional Ingredients: Functional foods are designed to provide additional health benefits beyond basic nutrition, incorporating ingredients like probiotics, antioxidants, and adaptogens. These foods support health, immunity, and mental well-being.

- Data-Driven Health Insights: Apps and platforms that analyse data from wearable devices allow consumers to receive dietary recommendations, meal planning, and food tracking to optimize their health.

- Example: Nutrigenomix, a genetic testing company, offers personalized nutrition recommendations based on an individual's DNA, helping consumers make food choices tailored to their unique health profiles. This approach exemplifies the potential for personalized nutrition to shape the future of food.

3. Culinary Tourism and Experiential Dining

Culinary tourism and experiential dining have grown as consumers seek immersive, memorable food experiences that go beyond simply dining out. These trends offer food businesses new ways to engage customers, from regional food tours to unique in-restaurant experiences.

- Local and Authentic Experiences: Consumers are increasingly interested in exploring regional and authentic cuisines, making culinary tourism popular. This trend supports local economies and promotes cultural exchange.

- Interactive and Themed Dining: Experiential dining, such as themed pop-ups, chef's table experiences, and cooking classes, appeals to customers looking for a unique, immersive food experience.

- Sustainability and Farm-to-Table: Many culinary tourism experiences emphasize sustainability and farm-to-table practices, highlighting local produce and artisanal methods to create authentic, eco-friendly experiences.

- Example: Outstanding in the Field is a traveling culinary experience that hosts farm-to-table dinners across the U.S. at scenic outdoor locations, allowing guests to enjoy meals sourced from local farms in unique settings. This experiential dining model has gained a dedicated following and supports local agriculture.

Strategic Planning for Adapting to Future Market Shifts

As the food industry continues to evolve, strategic planning enables food entrepreneurs to navigate uncertainty, anticipate trends, and prepare for change. Here are some effective approaches to adapting to future market shifts.

1. Trend Monitoring and Market Research

Staying informed about emerging trends, consumer preferences, and industry changes is essential for making proactive business decisions. Monitoring the market provides insights into what consumers are looking for, allowing businesses to adapt and stay competitive.

- Consumer Surveys and Feedback: Conducting regular surveys and gathering customer feedback helps businesses stay attuned to changing preferences and needs. Customer input provides valuable insights for product development and service improvements.
- Industry Reports and Research: Following industry reports, such as those from the National Restaurant Association or Technomic, provides data on trends and market predictions, helping businesses identify areas for innovation.
- Competitor Analysis: Monitoring competitors helps businesses understand their positioning, offerings, and responses to market shifts. Competitor analysis reveals gaps in the market and highlights opportunities for differentiation.
- Example: Whole Foods' annual trend report predicts food trends based on insights from industry experts and

consumer behaviour. This report has become a valuable resource for businesses looking to stay ahead of market changes.

2. Flexibility in Product Offerings and Menu Design

Flexibility is essential for adapting to changing market demands. Businesses that remain adaptable in their offerings, whether through seasonal menus, limited-time items, or product pivots, can respond effectively to shifting customer preferences.

- Seasonal and Limited-Time Items: Offering seasonal items or limited-time promotions keeps the menu fresh and encourages repeat visits. Seasonal offerings also align with trends in local sourcing and sustainability.
- Health-Conscious and Dietary Options: Catering to dietary preferences, such as gluten-free, vegan, or low-carb, helps businesses reach a wider customer base and respond to health trends.
- Innovative and Rotating Menus: Regularly updating the menu with new items or rotating options allows businesses to experiment with new flavours and respond to emerging culinary trends.

- Example: Taco Bell frequently releases limited-time items and seasonal flavours, which attract customers looking for variety and keep the brand relevant by aligning with current food trends.

3. Leveraging Technology for Adaptability

Technology enables businesses to streamline operations, respond to customer needs, and make data-driven decisions. Leveraging tools like data analytics, online ordering, and social media enhances flexibility and prepares businesses for future changes.

- Data-Driven Insights: Data analytics tools help businesses monitor sales trends, customer preferences, and operational efficiency. This information allows for informed decision-making and quick adjustments based on real-time insights.

- Online Ordering and Delivery: Expanding digital capabilities for online ordering, delivery, and curbside pickup improves customer access and prepares businesses to meet demand for convenience.

- Social Media and Digital Marketing: Social media platforms allow businesses to test new products, gather feedback, and promote menu updates directly to customers, fostering engagement and brand loyalty.

- Example: Sweetgreen uses data analytics to optimize inventory, track ingredient popularity, and adjust its menu based on customer demand. This approach enables Sweetgreen to remain agile and adapt quickly to shifts in consumer preferences.

4. Building Resilience with Sustainable and Ethical Practices

As sustainability becomes more important to consumers, businesses that prioritize eco-friendly practices are better positioned for long-term success. Sustainable practices build resilience, reduce costs, and appeal to customers who prioritize environmental responsibility.

- Local and Sustainable Sourcing: Using local suppliers reduces transportation costs, supports regional economies, and reduces environmental impact. Many customers also view local sourcing as a sign of quality and authenticity.

- Reducing Waste: Implementing waste reduction strategies, such as composting, recycling, and portion control, lowers costs and supports sustainability goals.

- Social Responsibility: Businesses that engage in ethical practices, such as fair labour and community involvement, build stronger customer relationships and demonstrate a commitment to positive social impact.

- Example: Blue Hill at Stone Barns has integrated farm-to-table practices, sourcing ingredients from its own farm and focusing on seasonal, sustainable cuisine. This approach supports environmental health, reduces waste, and aligns with consumer values around sustainability.

Final Insights on Cultivating a Resilient, Adaptable Business Mindset

For food entrepreneurs, preparing for the future means cultivating a mindset that embraces change, innovation, and resilience. This mindset is essential for navigating industry shifts, responding to challenges, and seizing opportunities in a dynamic market.

1. Embrace Innovation and Experimentation

Being open to innovation allows food businesses to explore new ideas, test concepts, and adapt to customer needs. Entrepreneurs who embrace experimentation are more likely to discover unique selling points, connect with diverse audiences, and differentiate themselves in the market.

- Pilot Programs and Test Runs: Testing new products,

services, or menu items on a small scale allows businesses to gauge customer response before a full rollout. This minimizes risk while fostering creativity.

- Staying Open to Change: The ability to pivot and adapt quickly to unexpected changes—whether due to market trends or economic shifts—strengthens resilience and prepares businesses for the unexpected.

- Example: Chipotle's "Chipotle Next Kitchen" concept allows the brand to test new ideas, like digital kitchens and drive-thru lanes, in select locations. This experimentation helps Chipotle adapt to changes in consumer behaviour.

2. Develop a Customer-Centric Approach

A customer-centric approach ensures that business decisions align with the needs, preferences, and expectations of the target audience. Listening to customer feedback and adapting offerings to meet their demands builds loyalty and strengthens the brand.

- Engage with Customers: Actively engaging with customers through surveys, social media, and reviews provides insights into their preferences and expectations.

- Personalization and Flexibility: Offering customized or flexible options, such as dietary modifications or build-your-own menus, creates a positive experience and appeals to a wider customer base.

- Example: Starbucks' mobile app collects customer data, allowing the brand to tailor promotions, offer recommendations, and create a personalized experience that resonates with loyal customers.

3. Prioritize Continuous Learning and Improvement

The food industry evolves rapidly, and successful entrepreneurs continuously seek new knowledge, skills, and perspectives. A commitment to learning—whether through industry conferences, training, or market research—ensures that businesses remain informed and ready to grow.

  - Professional Development: Attending industry events, workshops, and online courses helps entrepreneurs stay current on trends, technology, and best practices.
  - Learning from Data: Regularly analysing sales, customer feedback, and operational data provides insights that drive improvements in customer experience and efficiency.
  - Example: Whole Foods encourages employees to attend training programs that focus on topics like sustainability, customer service, and management, fostering a culture of learning that supports innovation and growth.

Building a Future-Ready Food Business

Preparing for the future of food entrepreneurship involves staying informed about trends, planning strategically, and cultivating a flexible, resilient mindset. As consumer preferences continue to evolve, food businesses that embrace sustainability, leverage technology, and focus on personalized experiences will be better positioned to thrive.

The examples of Beyond Meat, Sweetgreen, and Starbucks demonstrate the value of forward-thinking strategies in adapting to changing markets. By remaining adaptable, fostering innovation, and prioritizing customer needs, food entrepreneurs can build resilient, future-ready brands that succeed in an ever-evolving industry.

CONCLUSION

The journey through culinary entrepreneurship is as vibrant and diverse as the food industry itself. Throughout this book, we have explored the multifaceted aspects of starting, managing, and growing a food business, with each chapter offering insights into a specific area of this rewarding field. From conceptualizing a unique brand and identifying target markets to scaling operations and embracing innovation, each step brings food entrepreneurs closer to fulfilling their vision. Let's recap some essential lessons, offer encouragement to aspiring entrepreneurs, and reflect on the evolving nature of this industry.

Key Takeaways from Each Chapter

1. Introduction to Culinary Entrepreneurship
   - Culinary entrepreneurship is more than just cooking—it's about creating experiences, building connections, and delivering value to customers. Understanding the industry landscape and various business models sets a solid foundation for a successful venture.

2. The Culinary Entrepreneur's Mindset
   - Traits like resilience, creativity, adaptability, and

customer focus are essential for navigating challenges and seizing opportunities. Successful entrepreneurs combine these qualities with a passion for continuous learning and innovation.

3. Trends and Opportunities in the Food Industry
 - Staying attuned to trends such as sustainability, plant-based diets, and culinary tourism helps entrepreneurs identify emerging opportunities and align their business with evolving consumer values.

4. Exploring Business Models: From Restaurants to Food Trucks
 - Each food business model has unique benefits and challenges. Selecting the right model—whether a food truck, pop-up, or brick-and-mortar location—depends on budget, target audience, and operational preferences.

5. Conducting Market Research for Food Ventures
 - Understanding your target market, their preferences, and spending habits is crucial. Effective market research guides decision-making, from menu design to pricing and marketing strategies.

6. Formulating a Winning Concept
 - A successful food concept combines a cohesive theme, appealing menu, and brand identity that resonates with the target audience. Defining a clear, memorable concept helps attract loyal customers.

7. Business Plan Essentials for Food Entrepreneurs
 - A well-structured business plan provides direction and helps secure financing. Key components include the executive summary, market analysis, mission statement, and financial projections.

8. Funding Your Culinary Venture

- Funding options include personal savings, small business loans, investors, and crowdfunding. Each option has pros and cons, and the right choice depends on the entrepreneur's financial needs and goals.

9. Financial Planning and Budgeting

- Financial planning ensures long-term sustainability. Budgeting, cash flow management, and break-even analysis are vital tools for maintaining profitability and managing operational costs.

10. Navigating Legal and Regulatory Requirements

- Compliance with health codes, zoning laws, and food safety regulations is essential to operating legally and avoiding costly penalties. Legal compliance builds trust with customers and safeguards the business.

11. Location Strategy for Food Businesses

- Location affects visibility, accessibility, and customer traffic. Assessing foot traffic, competition, and local demand helps entrepreneurs choose a site that enhances brand reach and profitability.

12. Kitchen and Equipment Essentials

- A well-designed kitchen and reliable equipment improve efficiency and safety. Investing in quality equipment and planning an ergonomic layout are key to smooth operations.

13. Sourcing Ingredients and Supplier Management

- High-quality ingredients are fundamental to customer satisfaction. Building strong relationships with suppliers and considering factors like local sourcing and sustainability help maintain consistent product quality.

14. Menu Development and Pricing Strategy

- A thoughtfully curated menu aligns with brand identity and customer expectations. Pricing strategies should balance profitability with perceived value to attract and retain customers.

15. Managing Inventory and Minimizing Waste

- Effective inventory management controls costs and reduces waste. Techniques like tracking, forecasting, and repurposing surplus ingredients contribute to efficient operations and sustainability.

16. Hiring and Training a Stellar Team

- Employees play a critical role in the customer experience. Hiring for personality and skill, providing comprehensive training, and cultivating a positive workplace culture are essential for building a loyal, productive team.

17. Building a Brand in the Food Industry

- Brand identity encompasses visuals, storytelling, and values. A strong brand resonates with customers, builds loyalty, and differentiates the business in a competitive market.

18. Digital Marketing for Culinary Ventures

- Social media, SEO, and online reviews enhance visibility and engagement. Creating captivating content and interacting with followers help build a loyal online community.

19. Customer Experience and Relationship Management

- Exceptional service creates memorable experiences. Gathering feedback and implementing improvements build customer loyalty and enhance satisfaction.

20. Managing Reputation and Crisis Communications
 - Proactively managing online reviews and preparing for crises strengthens resilience. Transparent communication and accountability foster trust and help mitigate reputational damage.

21. Scaling Your Food Business
 - Scaling requires financial and operational readiness. Options like opening new locations, franchising, or launching product lines expand reach, but consistency and quality must be maintained.

22. Integrating Sustainable Practices
 - Sustainability benefits the environment, reduces costs, and aligns with consumer values. Eco-friendly sourcing, packaging, and waste reduction build a responsible brand.

23. Technology and Innovation in Food Entrepreneurship
 - Technology streamlines operations, improves customer engagement, and enhances data insights. POS systems, delivery apps, and data analytics are essential for modern food businesses.

24. Preparing for the Future of Food Entrepreneurship
 - Emerging trends like plant-based diets, personalized nutrition, and culinary tourism are shaping the industry. Strategic planning, flexibility, and resilience prepare entrepreneurs for future shifts.

Encouragement and Motivation for Aspiring Culinary Entrepreneurs

Starting and growing a food business is a journey filled

with both exciting opportunities and unique challenges. For aspiring culinary entrepreneurs, it's essential to remember that success doesn't happen overnight. Each step—whether it's creating a menu, choosing a location, or building a brand—contributes to your dream and moves you closer to your goals.

Resilience is key to overcoming obstacles, from financial constraints to unexpected operational hurdles. Each setback is a learning opportunity, an invitation to refine your approach and become a stronger entrepreneur. Keep the passion for your vision alive, stay curious, and never stop seeking inspiration from new sources, trends, and experiences. With commitment and hard work, you can turn your culinary vision into a thriving, impactful business that brings people together, creates memorable experiences, and contributes positively to the community.

Remember, the food industry is not just about serving meals; it's about creating moments, sharing cultures, and fostering connection. Every plate you serve, every customer you welcome, and every challenge you overcome is part of a greater story—your story as a culinary entrepreneur.

Final Words on the Evolving Nature of Culinary Entrepreneurship

Culinary entrepreneurship is constantly evolving. Consumer preferences, technological advancements, and global events reshape the industry, presenting both challenges and opportunities. Entrepreneurs who remain adaptable, innovative, and customer-focused will thrive in this ever-changing environment.

As you move forward, keep in mind that the food industry is not static. Trends will shift, technologies will advance, and new challenges will arise. Embrace change, be willing to reinvent your approach, and continuously seek ways to improve. Stay close to your customers, listen to their needs, and build a brand that resonates with their values. By remaining flexible and forward-thinking, you can create a business that stands the test of time.

The path of culinary entrepreneurship is one of creativity, resilience, and discovery. As you embark on or continue this journey, let your passion guide you, let your vision inspire you, and let your commitment drive you. With a focus on quality, community, and adaptability, you can create a culinary venture that not only succeeds but leaves a lasting impact on the industry and the people you serve.

Here's to your journey in the world of culinary entrepreneurship—may it be filled with success, growth, and endless inspiration.

EPILOGUE

The journey of culinary entrepreneurship is as dynamic and fulfilling as it is challenging. For those with a passion for food, community, and innovation, embarking on a culinary venture offers an opportunity to create memorable experiences, foster connections, and contribute positively to the ever-evolving food landscape. This book has journeyed through the essential elements of building a food business—from ideation, market research, and branding to operations, scaling, and preparing for the future. Each chapter has illustrated the practical steps, strategies, and insights that aspiring and established food entrepreneurs need to navigate this journey.

Yet, beyond these strategic steps, successful culinary entrepreneurship is defined by passion, resilience, and the courage to innovate. The food industry is one of constant change, driven by shifting consumer tastes, emerging technologies, and evolving societal values. As such, the most successful food entrepreneurs are not only skilled in managing the day-to-day operations of their business but are also visionary in adapting to the future, embracing sustainability, and championing innovation.

The Heart of Culinary Entrepreneurship: Passion,

Purpose, and People

At the heart of every thriving food business lies a powerful purpose. Whether it's providing a community with healthy meal options, sharing the rich flavours of a cherished cuisine, or supporting local farms and sustainable practices, purpose fuels the passion that drives success. This deeper purpose resonates with customers, employees, and partners, creating a sense of connection and loyalty that goes beyond a transactional relationship.

Moreover, the power of people cannot be overstated. The customer-centred approach, a recurring theme throughout this book, underscores the importance of creating experiences that leave a lasting impression. Culinary entrepreneurs who build their brands around customer needs and deliver exceptional service create a loyal base that champions their business, sharing it with friends, family, and social networks. But it's not just customers who matter—cultivating a team of motivated, skilled, and valued employees is equally vital. Employees who feel part of a mission are more likely to embody the brand's values, contributing to a positive workplace culture that reflects in customer interactions.

Innovation and Adaptability: Thriving in a Dynamic Industry

In the modern food industry, success is built upon adaptability and a willingness to innovate. This book has explored the vital role that technology, sustainability, and consumer trends play in shaping food businesses, and these elements are likely to continue evolving. The entrepreneurs who embrace this dynamism, who experiment with new ideas, and who remain agile are those best positioned to succeed in the long term.

From experimenting with plant-based foods to exploring personalized nutrition and engaging customers through digital platforms, innovation drives growth and relevance. By keeping an eye on trends and using data-driven insights, food businesses can remain connected to their customers' desires and adapt to their needs. In an industry that constantly reinvents itself, staying relevant means being open to change and consistently challenging the status quo.

Resilience and the Entrepreneurial Mindset

The road to culinary success is rarely straightforward. Every business will encounter setbacks, whether due to unforeseen operational challenges, economic fluctuations, or shifts in consumer preferences. What distinguishes a successful food entrepreneur is resilience —the ability to recover from challenges, learn from mistakes, and press forward with renewed commitment.

Building resilience begins with cultivating a mindset focused on growth and learning. Each challenge, each piece of feedback, and each new trend offers a chance to evolve and improve. By viewing obstacles as opportunities and maintaining a customer-focused vision, entrepreneurs can turn short-term setbacks into long-term success stories. Through persistence, adaptability, and a willingness to evolve, food entrepreneurs can transform their visions into enduring legacies.

The Lasting Impact of Culinary Entrepreneurship

Food is universal; it connects people, fosters tradition, and brings joy. Culinary entrepreneurs are uniquely positioned to make a positive impact—on individual lives, communities, and even the planet. By focusing on sustainable practices, supporting local economies, and creating spaces for community gathering, food businesses contribute to a vibrant food culture that benefits everyone involved.

Moreover, as society becomes more conscious of health, environmental impact, and ethical consumption, culinary entrepreneurs have the power to lead change. By championing responsible sourcing, reducing waste, and embracing environmentally-friendly practices, food businesses can promote a healthier, more sustainable world. Each step taken in the direction of sustainability, no matter how small, contributes to a better future and reflects the values of a conscientious and progressive business.

Looking Ahead: A Vision for the Future of Food

The future of food entrepreneurship is promising, filled with opportunities for those who are prepared to innovate, adapt, and lead with purpose. New technologies, sustainable practices, and consumer awareness continue to reshape the industry, presenting endless possibilities for food businesses to evolve and thrive. By staying informed, remaining adaptable, and prioritizing both customers and sustainability, today's food entrepreneurs can create businesses that endure and make a lasting impact.

As we close this journey, remember that culinary

entrepreneurship is as much an art as it is a science. While strategies, data, and best practices lay the groundwork for success, it is the unique vision, creativity, and resilience of each entrepreneur that bring a food business to life. May this book serve not only as a guide but as an inspiration for your journey in culinary entrepreneurship. The path ahead is yours to create, filled with flavours yet to be discovered, connections yet to be made, and dreams yet to be realized.

With dedication, a focus on community, and a commitment to innovation, you can build a food business that not only stands the test of time but also leaves a meaningful mark on the world. As you embark on this exciting path, remember that every meal served, every customer engaged, and every challenge overcome is part of the legacy you create in the world of food.

Thank you for joining on this journey—may your culinary venture be successful, impactful, and filled with the joy of sharing great food.

REFERENCES

1. Anderson, C. (2017). The Third Plate: Field Notes on the Future of Food. Penguin Books.
2. Barham, E., et al. (2012). The Local Food Movement: Definitions, Benefits, and Challenges. Journal of Sustainable Agriculture, 36(3), 289–310.
3. Bocken, N., Short, S., Rana, P., & Evans, S. (2014). A Literature and Practice Review to Develop Sustainable Business Model Archetypes. Journal of Cleaner Production, 65, 42–56.
4. Brown, C., & Miller, S. (2008). The Impacts of Local Markets: A Review of Research on Farmers Markets and Community Supported Agriculture (CSA). American Journal of Agricultural Economics, 90(5), 1296–1302.
5. Byrne, A., & Hart, T. (2015). Culinary Tourism and Local Food Trends. In T. Jamal & M. Robinson (Eds.), The SAGE Handbook of Tourism Studies (pp. 233–251). SAGE Publications.
6. Camillo, A. (2015). Handbook of Research on Global Hospitality and Tourism Management. IGI Global.
7. Duhigg, C. (2012). The Power of Habit: Why We Do What We Do in Life and Business. Random House.
8. Galloway, S. (2018). The Four: The Hidden DNA of Amazon, Apple, Facebook, and Google. Portfolio.
9. Gunders, D., Bloom, J., & Spiker, M. (2017). Wasted: How

America Is Losing Up to 40 Percent of Its Food from Farm to Fork to Landfill. Natural Resources Defense Council.

10. Inwood, S. M., & Sharp, J. S. (2012). Farmers' Market Locations and their Perceived Impacts on Economic Success. Journal of Agriculture, Food Systems, and Community Development, 2(2), 15–30.

11. James, A., & Lahti, L. (2020). Sustainability in the Restaurant Industry: A Systematic Review. International Journal of Hospitality Management, 87, 102–113.

12. Kimes, S. E., & Laing, J. (2011). Restaurant Revenue Management: Practical Strategies for Maximizing Profit and Efficiency. Cornell Hospitality Report, 11(2), 4–16.

13. Kotler, P., & Keller, K. L. (2015). Marketing Management (15th ed.). Pearson.

14. Lavelle, M. (2017). Tracking the Growth of Food Tourism in Global Markets. Journal of Culinary Science & Technology, 12(3), 367–384.

15. Lee, C., & Levy, S. (2021). Digital Transformation in Food and Beverage: Navigating Technological Advancements for Success. Journal of Digital Business, 19(4), 456–479.

16. Mintel Group. (2022). Global Food Trends 2022 Report. Mintel.

17. National Restaurant Association. (2021). State of the Restaurant Industry Report. National Restaurant Association.

18. Pietrykowski, B. (2018). You Are What You Eat: Food, Culture, and Identity. Routledge.

19. Pollan, M. (2006). The Omnivore's Dilemma: A Natural History of Four Meals. Penguin Books.

20. Ritzer, G. (2015). The McDonaldization of Society. SAGE Publications.

21. Schlosser, E. (2001). Fast Food Nation: The Dark Side

of the All-American Meal. Houghton Mifflin.

22. Simon, M. (2010). Appetite for Profit: How the Food Industry Undermines Our Health and How to Fight Back. Nation Books.

23. Sustainability Accounting Standards Board (SASB). (2018). Food and Beverage Sector Standards. SASB.

24. Thaler, R. H., & Sunstein, C. R. (2009). Nudge: Improving Decisions about Health, Wealth, and Happiness. Penguin Books.

25. World Economic Forum. (2021). Future of Food Systems: Innovations, Investments, and Partnerships. World Economic Forum.

26. Zepeda, L., & Deal, D. (2009). Organic and Local Food Consumer Behavior: Survey Results from a Wisconsin Farmers Market. Renewable Agriculture and Food Systems, 24(4), 326–334.

27. Zimmerman, E. A., & Reif, A. (2014). Sustainable Restaurant Operations: A Guide for Food and Beverage Managers. Wiley & Sons.

This list draws on seminal texts, industry reports, and academic journals that provide a comprehensive foundation for understanding culinary entrepreneurship, sustainable practices, digital innovation, and consumer trends within the food industry. These resources offer practical insights and scholarly perspectives, supporting the book's exploration of both foundational strategies and emerging trends in the dynamic world of food entrepreneurship.

GLOSSARY OF TERMS

Adaptability
The ability of a business or individual to change or adjust in response to evolving circumstances, customer needs, or market trends. Essential for staying competitive in the dynamic food industry.

Alternative Proteins
Non-traditional protein sources, such as plant-based, lab-grown, or insect-derived proteins, that serve as substitutes for animal proteins. Popular in the rise of plant-based diets and sustainability-focused menus.

Ambiance
The atmosphere or mood of a food establishment, created through elements such as decor, lighting, music, and layout. A key component of the customer experience that influences perception and enjoyment.

Brand Identity
The unique personality of a business, defined by its name, logo, design, and communication style. A strong brand identity helps differentiate a business and foster customer loyalty.

Culinary Tourism
A type of tourism that focuses on exploring food and drink experiences, often involving local cuisine, food festivals, and immersive dining experiences. Culinary tourism highlights food as a central aspect of cultural exploration.

Customer Experience (CX)
The overall perception and feelings that customers have when interacting with a business. CX encompasses service, ambiance, product quality, and every touchpoint that influences satisfaction and loyalty.

Digital Transformation
The adoption of digital tools and technologies to improve operations, customer engagement, and business growth. In the food industry, this includes online ordering, data analytics, and social media marketing.

Eco-Friendly
Practices that are environmentally conscious and reduce harm to the environment. Eco-friendly initiatives in the food industry often involve sustainable sourcing, waste reduction, and biodegradable packaging.

Experiential Dining
A dining approach that emphasizes unique, memorable experiences beyond food, such as themed decor, interactive elements, and storytelling. Experiential dining aims to engage multiple senses and create lasting impressions.

Farm-to-Table
A food movement that promotes sourcing ingredients directly from local farms and producers to ensure

freshness, reduce environmental impact, and support the local economy. Farm-to-table practices emphasize sustainability and quality.

Food Safety
Practices and procedures that ensure food is safe to consume, including hygiene standards, handling protocols, and compliance with health codes. Food safety is critical to customer trust and regulatory compliance.

Franchising
A business model in which a brand (the franchisor) licenses its name, operations, and products to independent operators (franchisees) in exchange for fees. Franchising allows rapid expansion with less direct investment.

Functional Foods
Foods that offer health benefits beyond basic nutrition, often containing ingredients like antioxidants, probiotics, or vitamins. Functional foods are part of the growing trend toward health-conscious eating.

Inventory Management
The process of overseeing the ordering, storage, and use of ingredients and supplies. Effective inventory management helps control costs, reduce waste, and ensure that products are always available for customers.

Loyalty Program
A marketing strategy that rewards repeat customers with benefits such as discounts, freebies, or exclusive access. Loyalty programs encourage customer retention and foster long-term relationships.

Market Research

The process of gathering and analysing information about target customers, competitors, and market trends. Market research helps businesses make informed decisions about products, pricing, and branding.

Personalized Nutrition
Tailored dietary recommendations based on an individual's unique health needs, preferences, or genetic profile. Personalized nutrition is gaining traction as consumers seek customized health solutions.

Point of Sale (POS)
A system used to process sales transactions, often integrating with inventory, analytics, and customer management tools. Modern POS systems streamline operations and provide valuable data insights.

Product Line Expansion
The strategy of adding new products or variations to an existing line to reach new customers or enhance brand offerings. In food businesses, product line expansion may include bottled sauces, packaged snacks, or meal kits.

Sourcing
The process of selecting suppliers and acquiring ingredients, typically based on criteria like quality, cost, and sustainability. Sourcing decisions impact both product quality and a brand's ethical reputation.

Sustainability
Practices that minimize environmental impact and support long-term ecological health. In the food industry, sustainability efforts include eco-friendly packaging, reducing waste, and supporting local producers.

Target Market

A specific group of consumers that a business aims to reach based on demographics, preferences, and behaviours. Understanding the target market helps shape product offerings, marketing strategies, and customer engagement.

Technology Integration
The use of digital tools and systems within a business to improve efficiency, streamline processes, and enhance customer service. In the food industry, technology integration includes POS systems, online ordering, and mobile apps.

Value Proposition
The unique value a business offers to its customers, often highlighting what differentiates it from competitors. A clear value proposition attracts customers by addressing their specific needs and desires.

Waste Reduction
Strategies to minimize waste generated in food production and service, such as composting, portion control, and recycling. Waste reduction supports sustainability goals and improves cost-efficiency.

Workplace Culture
The values, behaviours, and practices that define the work environment in a business. Positive workplace culture fosters employee satisfaction, retention, and productivity, benefiting the overall customer experience.

This glossary provides concise definitions of key terms that are essential to understanding culinary entrepreneurship. From technical processes like inventory management to broader concepts such as sustainability and customer experience, these terms capture the unique elements and challenges that food entrepreneurs encounter in building a successful business.

ACKNOWLEDGMENTS

Writing Culinary Entrepreneurship: Starting and Managing Food Businesses has been a journey filled with invaluable insights, support, and inspiration from numerous individuals. First and foremost, I am deeply grateful to the culinary entrepreneurs, chefs, and business professionals whose stories and experiences have shaped this book. Your commitment to creativity, resilience, and innovation has been a guiding force.

I would like to express my appreciation to Irene Minds for their unwavering support, vision, and dedication in bringing this project to life. Thank you for believing in this book and for providing the platform and guidance to make it accessible to readers everywhere.

To my family and friends, thank you for your endless encouragement and for understanding the time and dedication it took to complete this work. Your patience and faith in me have been a constant source of motivation. Special thanks to my colleagues and mentors who have generously shared their expertise, helping shape the perspectives and depth presented in this book.

Finally, to all readers—whether you are just beginning your journey in culinary entrepreneurship or are seasoned professionals—thank you for allowing me to be part of your growth and success. It is my hope that this book serves as a trusted companion and inspires you to pursue your vision with passion and resilience.

Thank you.

COPYRIGHT INFORMATION

Culinary Entrepreneurship: Starting and Managing Food Businesses
© 2024 Dr Bhaskar Bora
Published by Irene Minds

All rights reserved. No part of this book may be reproduced, distributed, or transmitted in any form or by any means, including photocopying, recording, or other electronic or mechanical methods, without the prior written permission of the publisher, except in the case of brief quotations embodied in critical reviews and certain other non-commercial uses permitted by copyright law.

For permission requests, please contact the author at bora.dr@gmail.com.

DISCLAIMER

The information provided in Culinary Entrepreneurship: Starting and Managing Food Businesses is based on research, industry practices, and the author's experience. This book is intended for informational purposes only and should not be considered a substitute for professional advice. While every effort has been made to ensure the accuracy and completeness of the information contained herein, the author and publisher assume no responsibility or liability for errors, omissions, or interpretations of the information contained in this book.

Readers are encouraged to consult appropriate professionals before making any business or financial decisions. The author and publisher specifically disclaim any liability for any direct or indirect losses that may result from the application of information contained in this book.

www.ingramcontent.com/pod-product-compliance
Lightning Source LLC
Chambersburg PA
CBHW071447220526
45472CB00003B/702